Quantitative Management

For further volumes:
http://www.springer.com/series/10621

Gang Kou • Daji Ergu • Yi Peng • Yong Shi

Data Processing for the AHP/ANP

 Springer

Gang Kou
School of Management and Economics
University of Electronic Science
   and Technology of China
North Jianshe Road
Chengdu
China, People's Republic

Daji Ergu
College of Electrical and Information
   Engineering
Southwest University for Nationalities
Yihuan Road
Chengdu
China, People's Republic

Yi Peng
School of Managment and Economics
University of Electronic Science
   and Technology of China
North Jianshe Road
Chengdu
China, People's Republic

Yong Shi
University of Nebraska at Omaha IS&T
Dodge Street
Omaha Nebraska
USA

ISSN 2194-086X   ISSN 2194-0878 (electronic)
ISBN 978-3-642-29212-5   ISBN 978-3-642-29213-2 (eBook)
DOI 10.1007/978-3-642-29213-2
Springer Heidelberg New York Dordrecht London

Library of Congress Control Number: 2012944253

Printed on acid-free paper

Springer is part of Springer Science+Business Media (www.springer.com)

Abstract

The positive reciprocal pairwise comparison matrix (PCM) is a well established technique and widely used in multiple criteria decision making (MCDM) methods to perform pairwise comparisons and derive the weight vectors of being compared items, especially in the analytical hierarchy (network) process (AHP/ANP). The PCM is also used to quantify the qualitative and/or intangible attributes into measurable quantities. Consistency test, inconsistent data identification and adjustment, missing or uncertain data estimation, and sensitivity analysis of rank reversal are important research issues in this field. Although these issues have been extensively studied, there is no universally accepted, simple and generalized data processing model to handle the above mentioned issues simultaneously. In this book, the maximum eigenvalue threshold method is proposed as the new consistency index for the AHP/ANP. An induced bias matrix model (IBMM) is proposed to identify and adjust the inconsistent data, and estimate the missing or uncertain data. Based on the IBMM, several questionnaire design improvement formats are proposed to quickly collect the data to make rapid and efficient decision making. Besides, the IBMM is further used to analyze the sensitivity of rank reversal issue when adding new criteria or alternatives or deleting old criteria or alternatives. Finally, two applications of IBMM, task scheduling and resource allocation in cloud computing environment, and risk assessment and decision analysis, are used to illustrate the proposed IBMM. As an extended model of IBMM, an induced arithmetic average bias matrix (IAABM) is described in detail in final Chapter.

Keywords

The analytical hierarchy (network) process (AHP/ANP), Induced bias matrix model (IBMM), Data processing, Consistency test, Maximum eigenvalue threshold, Inconsistency identification and adjustment, Uncertain or missing values estimation, Rank reversal, Induced arithmetic average bias matrix (IAABM).

Contents

Chapter 1
Introduction

In complex decision making environment, decision making usually involves tangible and intangible multiple criteria and alternatives to choose from. To deal with such qualitative and quantitative factors in multiple criteria decision making (MCDM), in 1970s, Saaty (1978, 1979, 1980) proposed an Analytical Hierarchy Process (AHP). Since then, this method has been extensively applied into many real applications, for instance in manufacturing systems (Li and Huang 2009), quality consultants (Cebeci and Ruan 2007), software evaluation (Cebeci 2009; Peng et al. 2011a), supplier evaluation and selection (Akarte et al. 2001; Handfield et al. 2002; Chan 2003; Bayazit 2006; Chamodrakas et al. 2010; Labib 2011), strategy selection (Li and Li 2009; Chen and Wang 2010), weapon selection (Dagdeviren et al. 2009), project selection (Enea and Piazza 2004; Amiri 2010).

During the process of decision making, especially for some complex decision making problems, it is preferred to compare two criteria/attributes at one time than to compare several criteria/attributes simultaneously. Therefore, the pairwise comparison technique, originally proposed by Thurstone (1927), is creatively used in the analytical hierarchy process (AHP) to pairwise compare and determine the relative importance of two attributes or alternatives with respect to a given criterion. All pairwise comparisons are then arranged in a matrix $A = (a_{ij})_{n \times n}$, and popularly called pairwise comparison matrix (PCM hereinafter) in literature. A PCM is sometimes called a positive reciprocal matrix since it should satisfy the positive reciprocal property: $a_{ij} = 1/a_{ji}, a_{ij} > 0$ for all i and j. In addition to the positive reciprocal property, a PCM is said to be perfectly consistent if it satisfies the relationship: $a_{ij} = a_{ik}a_{kj}$ for all i, j and k, which is often called cardinal consistent condition.

The PCM usually consists of elements expressed on a numerical scale to quantify the qualitative decision problem. Therefore, the first issue for a PCM is that how to develop a scale to transfer the linguistic description to the numerical values, including 9-point Ratio Scale introduced by Saaty (1978), Differences Scale proposed by Triantaphyllou and Mann (1995) and the Exponential Scales developed by Lootsma (1988, 1991) etc.

G. Kou et al., *Data Processing for the AHP/ANP*, Quantitative Management 1,
DOI 10.1007/978-3-642-29213-2_1, © Springer-Verlag Berlin Heidelberg 2013

The values of elements in a PCM are given by decision makers based on their experiences and expertise, thus the pairwise comparison matrix (PCM) could be inconsistent due to the limitations of decision makers' experiences and expertise as well as the complexity nature of the decision problem. For instance, assume we have three comparison alternatives A, B and C, if A is preferred to B m times, and B is preferred to C n times, but A is not preferred to C mn times, which violates the aforementioned cardinal consistent condition, and called cardinal inconsistency. However, if A is just preferred to B, and B is just preferred to C, but A is not preferred to C, then it is called ordinal inconsistency. In this book, we mainly focus on the cardinal inconsistency issue, and in general, say it inconsistency. It is unrealistic to obtain a perfectly consistent PCM in practice, therefore, AHP allows a certain level of inconsistency of the PCM, which is measured by the consistency ratio (CR) (Saaty 1980), that is, $CR = CI/RI < 0.1$, where the Consistency Index $CI = (\lambda_{max} - n)/(n - 1)$, RI is the average Random Index based on Matrix Size n, λ_{max} is the maximum eigenvalue of matrix A (Saaty 1991). If the CR < 0.1, then the PCM is said to be of acceptable consistency indicating the inconsistency is relatively small, otherwise the inconsistent elements should be identified and adjusted in order to make a valid decision. However, as the CR method itself can not identify the most inconsistent elements, Koczkodaj (1993) proposed a new consistency measure CM, based on the properties of basic comparison matrices of 3rd order. Peláez and Lamata (2003) developed a method based on the determinant of the matrix. Besides, the threshold value of 0.1 has received criticisms since it lacks a meaningful interpretation. For instance, Aguarón and Moreno-Jiménez (2003) proposed different thresholds for the matrices with different orders to provide an interpretation of the inconsistency threshold analogous to the CR = 10%, that is, 0.3147 for n = 3, 0.3526 for n = 4 and 0.370 for n > 4. Alonso and Lamata (2006) formulated a regression of the random indices of maximum eigenvalue. Besides, many statistical approaches for consistency test in AHP have also been proposed (Moreno and Vargas 1993; Vargas 2008).

In an $n \times n$ PCM, the decision makers have to make $n(n-1)/2$ comparisons to get a complete PCM. Once the PCM is determined, the final priority vector of the decision making problems can be derived by the following several methods: Eigenvector Method (Saaty 1977), Normalization of the Column Sum Method and Arithmetic Mean of Normalized Columns Method (Saaty 1980), the Direct Least Squares Method (DLSM) and the Weighted Least Squares Method (WLSM) (Chu et al. 1979), the Logarithmic Least Squares Method (LLSM) (Crawford and Williams 1985), the Logarithmic Goal Programming Method (LGPM) (Bryson 1995), Geometric Means Solution (GMS) (Barzilai 1997) and so on. Excellent review of these methods can be found in Choo and Wedley (2004) and Lin (2007).

In AHP, the calculated priorities are plausible only if the pairwise comparison matrices pass the consistency test, when the transitivity and reciprocity rules are respected within the pairwise comparison process (Ishizaka and Lusti 2004). However, the data of a PCM are usually collected and used to assign criteria weights or scores of alternatives through questionnaire survey, and as the surveyed experts are often biased in their subjective comparisons, the inconsistent comparisons of preference judgment may exist in a PCM. Therefore, the inconsistency issues in AHP have been widely studied, and a number of approaches and models are proposed and developed (Saaty 1986, 1987, 1990; Harker and Vargas 1987; Liu 1999; Xu and Wei 1999; Wei and Zhang 2000; Li and Ma 2007; Cao et al. 2008; Iida 2009; Koczkodaj and Szarek 2010). However, some existing methods are complicated and difficult to use in the revising process of the inconsistent comparison matrix while some are difficult to preserve most of the original comparison information since a new matrix has to be constructed to replace the original comparison matrix (Ergu et al. 2011b). In addition, most of the methods are based on the priority vectors derived from the inconsistent matrix. For instance, Harker and Vargas (1987) derived the formula, $\partial \lambda_{max}/\partial a_{ij} = v_i \omega_j - a_{ji}^2 v_j \omega_i$, to identify the most inconsistent entry by examining (any) one of the largest absolute value in the $n(n-1)/2$ values $\{v_i \omega_j - a_{ji}^2 v_j \omega_i\}$, $i > j$. In Saaty (1980, 1994), the matrix $B = [|a_{ij} - \omega_i/\omega_j|]$ of absolute differences was constructed to identify the most inconsistent element. In the AHP Expert Choice software, a similar matrix, $E = (\varepsilon_{ij}) = (a_{ij}\omega_j/\omega_i)$, is constructed to identify the most inconsistent element, where ω_i and ω_j are underlying subjective priority weights belonging to a priority vector $\omega = (\omega_1, \ldots, \omega_n)$ (Saaty 2003). Two similar methods are proposed by Xu and Wei (1999) and Cao et al. (2008) to detect the inconsistencies.

In addition to the inconsistency issue in the AHP, it is difficult for experts to assign the values to every comparison matrix for a complex decision problem. Besides, it is sometimes impossible to get complete comparison matrices due to the limited expertise, time pressure, and preference conflicts (Harker and Vargas 1987; Forman 1990). On the other hand, the PCM must be complete in order to derive the final priority vectors. If a PCM is incomplete, the missing entries should be filled with values that can keep or improve the PCM consistency. Hence, the issues on how to deal with such incomplete reciprocal or fuzzy PCM with missing entries have been investigated extensively (Carmone et al. 1997; Alonso et al. 2004, 2008; Hu and Tsai 2006; Brunelli et al. 2007; Fedrizzi and Giove 2007; Chiclana et al. 2009).

Apart from the PCM and the consistency test, there are several assumptions when the AHP is applied to make decisions, such as, the independence between higher level elements and lower level elements, the independence of the elements within a level, and the hierarchy structure of the decision problem (Saaty 1994; Saaty and Zoffer 2011). However, in reality, decision makers are often facing complicated decision problems which can not be structured hierarchically. Furthermore, the interactions of decision attributes within the same level and the feedbacks between two different levels are important issues that should be considered during the decision making process. Therefore, the AHP method does not work accurately when solving such decision problems (Saaty 1996).

The analytical network process (ANP), as an extensive and complementary method of the AHP, was introduced and further developed by Saaty (1996, 1999, 2001a, b, 2003, 2004, 2005, 2006, 2008). The ANP method can be used to make decision problems which cannot be structured hierarchically and doesn't have the inner-independent and outer-independent assumptions. Since its introduction, the ANP method is gaining popularity and applied to diverse areas. For instance, Lee and Kim (2000) suggested an improved information system (IS) project selection method using the ANP within a zero–one goal programming model to solve the IS project selection problems. Hafeez et al. (2002) provided a structured framework for determining the key capabilities of a firm using the ANP. Karsak et al. (2003) employed the ANP to evaluate the interrelationships among customer needs and product technical requirements (PTRs) while determining the importance levels of PTRs in the house of quality (HOQ). Niemira and Saaty (2004) developed an imbalance-crisis turning point model to forecast the likelihood of a financial crisis based on an ANP framework. Chung et al. (2005) employed the ANP to select and evaluate different product mixes in a semiconductor fabricator. Kahraman et al. (2006) used the ANP to obtain the coefficients of the objective function and proposed a fuzzy optimization model for Quality function deployment (QFD) planning process using the ANP. Bayazit and Karpak (2007) developed an ANP based framework to assess the implementation of total quality management (TQM). Wu (2008) proposed an effective solution based on a combined ANP and DEMATEL approach to help companies evaluating and selecting their knowledge management (KM) strategies. Aktar and Ustun (2009) suggested an integrated approach of Archimedean Goal Programming (AGP) and Analytic Network Process (ANP) to evaluate the suppliers and determine their periodic shipment allocations given a number of tangible and intangible criteria. Caballero-Luque et al. (2010) presented a model based on the ANP to help organization managers to verify if their website contents are appropriate for satisfying the goals they have established.

In addition to the above fields, the ANP has also widely been used in risk assessment and decision analysis. For instance, Lu et al. (2007) applied the ANP to deal with the degree of risk for the main activities of an urban bridge project. Raisinghani et al. (2007) utilized the ANP to provide insight into optimum-seeking decision processes by managers and study the "systems with feedback" where the e-commerce strategy may both dominate and be dominated directly and indirectly by the business-level strategy. Dagdeviren et al. (2008) employed the ANP to identify the faulty behavior risk (FBR) which is significant in work system safety. Besides, Levy and Taji (2007) proposed a Group Analytic Network Process (GANP) approach to support hazards planning and emergency management under incomplete information.

In the ANP, similar to the AHP, three issues need to be solved for a pairwise comparison matrix (PCM): consistency test, inconsistent element(s) identification and adjustment, and missing values estimation. However, these issues are more complicated in the ANP than in the AHP since there are more comparison matrices in the ANP. In addition, although the above reviewed heuristics and approximations of comparison matrix do not affect the priority order and may achieve consistent result in AHP, they are not acceptable in the Analytic Network Process (ANP). In general, there are more pairwise comparison matrices in ANP than AHP, and all ratio scale priority vectors are columns in supermatrix in ANP (Saaty 1996, 2006; Caballero-Luque et al. 2010). The priority result of ANP changes even if the pair-wise comparison matrices are slightly inconsistent (Saaty 1996, 2005; Lee and Kim 2000; Mikhailov and Singh 2003). Therefore, an inconsistency identification method that can retain most of the comparison information in the original pair-wise comparison matrix provided by the experts is a requisite for ANP and AHP.

In summary, the data of PCM both in AHP and ANP usually involve in consistency test index, inconsistency identification, missing values estimation, questionnaire design for collecting surveyed data and rank reversal issues. To process the understudied issues of data in the PCM, Ergu et al. (2011a) proposed a maximum eigenvalue threshold method, which is mathematically equivalent to the consistency ratio method as the new consistency index for the AHP/ANP. To identify the inconsistent elements simply and accurately while preserving most of the original comparison information in the PCM, an induced bias matrix model (*IBMM*), which is only based on the original comparison matrix and independent to the way of deriving the priority weight vectors, was proposed in Ergu et al. (2011b). The *IBMM* is further extended to estimate the missing item scores of the PCM whilst keep the global consistency in Ergu et al. (2011c), and to optimize the questionnaire design in Ergu and Kou (2011). Besides, the proposed *IBMM* is applied to two real cases in Ergu et al. (2011d, e): task-oriented resource allocation in cloud computing environment and risk assessment and decision analysis for improving the consistency ratios of the PCMs. Finally, another form of IBMM, the induced arithmetic average bias matrix (IAABM), is further introduced in Ergu and Kou (2012), which are simpler and easier than existing methods.

The remaining parts of this book are organized as follows: Chap. 2 describes the maximum eigenvalue threshold method for AHP/ANP. The basics of the IBMM for processing the data of the PCM in AHP/ANP are presented in detail in the Chap. 3. The IBMM is extended to estimate the missing values in Chap. 4. Chapter 5 introduces the IBMM for optimizing the questionnaire design and estimating the missing items scores. Chapter 6 briefly describes the process of sensitivity analysis of rank reversal by IBMM. Two real world applications of IBMM are studied in Chap. 7. Chapter 8 briefly presents the IAABM, an extension of IBMM.

References

Aguarón J, Moreno-Jiménez J (2003) The geometric consistency index: approximated thresholds. Eur J Oper Res 147:137–145

Akarte MM, Surendra NV, Ravi B, Rangaraj N (2001) Web based casting supplier evaluation using analytical hierarchy process. J Oper Res Soc 52(5):511–522

Aktar DE, Ustun O (2009) Analytic network process and multi-period goal programming integration in purchasing decisions. Comput Ind Eng 56(2):677–690

Alonso J, Lamata T (2006) Consistency in the analytic hierarchy process: a new approach. Int J Uncert, Fuzz Knowl-Based Syst 14:445–459

Alonso S, Chiclana F, Herrera F, Herrera-Viedma E (2004) A learning procedure to estimate missing values in fuzzy preference relations based on additive consistency. In: Torra V, Narukawa Y (eds) MDAI 2004. Springer, Berlin/Heidelberg, pp 227–238

Alonso S, Chiclana F, Herrera F, Herrera-Viedma E (2008) A consistency-based procedure to estimate missing pairwise preference values. Int J Intell Syst 23:155–175

Amiri MP (2010) Project selection for oil-fields development by using the AHP and fuzzy TOPSIS methods. Expert Syst Appl 37(9):6218–6224

Barzilai J (1997) Deriving weights from pairwise comparison matrices. J Opl Res Soc 48:1226–1232

Bayazit O (2006) Use of analytic network process in vendor selection decisions. Benchmark Int J 13(5):566–579

Bayazit O, Karpak B (2007) An analytical network process-based framework for successful total quality management (TQM): an assessment of Turkish manufacturing industry readiness. Int J Prod Econ 105(1):79–96

Brunelli M, Fedrizzi M, Giove S (2007) Reconstruction methods for incomplete fuzzy preference relations: a numerical comparison. In: Masulli F, Mitra S, Pasi G (eds) WILF 2007, LNAI, 2007. Springer, Berlin/Heidelberg, pp 86–93

Bryson N (1995) A goal programming method for generating priority vectors. J Opl Res Soc 46:641–648

Caballero-Luque A, Aragonés-Beltrán P, García-Melón M, Dema-Pérez C (2010) Analysis of the alignment of company goals to web content using ANP. Int J Inf Technol Decis Mak 9(3):419–436

Cao D, Leung LC, Law JS (2008) Modifying inconsistent comparison matrix in analytic hierarchy process: a heuristic approach. Decis Supp Syst 44:944–953

Carmone FJ, Kara A, Zanakis SH (1997) A Monte Carlo investigation of incomplete pairwise comparison matrices in AHP. Eur J Oper Res 102(3):538–553

Cebeci U (2009) Fuzzy AHP-based decision support system for selecting ERP systems in textile industry by using balanced scorecard. Expert Syst Appl 36:8900–8909

Cebeci U, Ruan D (2007) A multi-attribute comparison of Turkish quality consultants by fuzzy AHP. Int J Inf Technol Decis Mak 6(1):191–207

Chamodrakas I, Batis D, Martakos D (2010) Supplier selection in electronic marketplaces using satisficing and fuzzy AHP. Expert Syst Appl 37:490–498

Chan FTS (2003) Interactive selection model for supplier selection process: an analytical hierarchy process approach. Int J Prod Res 41(15):3549–3579

Chen MK, Wang S-C (2010) The critical factors of success for information service industry in developing international market: using analytic hierarchy process (AHP) approach. Expert Syst Appl 37:694–704

Chiclana F, Herrera-Viedma E, Alonso S (2009) A note on two methods for estimating missing pairwise preference values. IEEE Trans Syst Man Cybernet B Cybernet 39:1628–1633

Choo E, Wedley W (2004) A common framework for deriving preference values from pairwise comparison matrices. Comput Oper Res 31(6):893–908

Chu A, Kalaba R, Springam K (1979) A comparison of two methods for determining the weights of belonging to fuzzy sets. J Opt Theory Appl 27:531–541

Chung SH, Lee AHI, Pearn WL (2005) Analytic network process (ANP) approach for product mix planning in semiconductor fabricator. Int J Prod Econ 96(1):15–36

Crawford G, Williams C (1985) A note on the analysis of subjective judgment matrices. J Math Psychol 29:387–405

Dagdeviren M, Yuksel I, Kurt M (2008) A fuzzy analytic network process (ANP) model to identify faulty behavior risk (FBR) in work system. Safety Sci 46(5):771–783

Dagdeviren M, Yavuz S, Killnç N (2009) Weapon selection using the AHP and TOPSIS methods under fuzzy environment. Expert Syst Appl 36:8143–8151

Enea M, Piazza T (2004) Project selection by constrained fuzzy AHP. Fuzzy Optimiz Decis Mak 3:39–62

Ergu D, Kou G (2011) Questionnaire design improvement and missing item scores estimation for rapid and efficient decision making. Ann Oper Res 2011. doi:10.1007/s10479-011-0922-3

Ergu D, Kou G (2012) IAABM for consistency test in pairwise comparison matrix. Information

Ergu D, Kou G, Peng Y, Shi Y (2011a) A new consistency index for comparison matrices in the ANP, New State of MCDM in the 21st Century. Lecture notes in economics and mathematical systems, vol 648, part 1, pp 47–56

Ergu D, Kou G, Peng Y, Shi Y (2011b) A simple method to improve the consistency ratio of the pair-wise comparison matrix in ANP. Eur J Oper Res 213(1):246–259. doi:10.1016/j.ejor.2011.03.014

Ergu D, Kou G, Peng Y, Shi Y, Shi Yu (2011c) BIMM: a bias induced matrix model for incomplete reciprocal pairwise comparison matrix. J Multi-Crit Decis Anal. doi:10.1002/mcda.472

Ergu D, Kou G, Peng Y, Shi Y, Shi Yu (2011d) The analytic hierarchy process: task scheduling and resource allocation in cloud computing environment. J Supercomput. doi:10.1007/s11227-011-0625-1

Ergu D, Kou G, Shi Y, Shi Yu (2011e) Analytic network process in risk assessment and decision analysis. Comput Oper Res. doi:10.1016/j.cor.2011.03.005

Fedrizzi M, Giove S (2007) Incomplete pairwise comparison and consistency optimization. Eur J Oper Res, Elsevier, 183(1):303–313

Forman EH (1990) Random indices for incomplete pairwise comparison matrices. Eur J Oper Res 48(1):153–155

Hafeez K, Zhang Y, Malak N (2002) Determining key capabilities of a firm using analytic hierarchy process. Int J Prod Econ 76(1):39–51

Handfield R, Walton SV, Sroufe R, Melnyk SA (2002) Applying environmental criteria to supplier assessment: a study in the application of the analytical hierarchy process. Eur J Oper Res 141(1):70–87

Harker P, Vargas L (1987) The theory of ratio scale estimation: Saaty's analytic hierarchy process. Manage Sci 33(11):1383–1403

Hu Y-C, Tsai J-F (2006) Backpropagation multi-layer perception for incomplete pairwise comparison matrices in analytic hierarchy process. Appl Math Comput 180(1):53–62

Iida Y (2009) Ordinality consistency test about items and notation of a pairwise comparison matrix in AHP. In: Proceedings of the international symposium on the Analytic Hierarchy Process

Ishizaka A, Lusti M (2004) An expert module to improve the consistency of AHP matrices. Int Trans Oper Res 11:97–105. doi:10.1111/j.1475-3995.2004.00443.x

Kahraman C, Ertay T, Buyukozkan G (2006) A fuzzy optimization model for QFD planning process using analytic network approach. Eur J Oper Res 171(2):390–411

Karsak EE, Sozer S, Alptekin SE (2003) Product planning in quality function deployment using a combined analytic network process and goal programming approach. Comput Ind Eng 44(1):171–190

Koczkodaj WW (1993) A new definition of consistency of pairwise comparisons. Math Comput Model 18(7):79–84

Koczkodaj WW, Szarek SJ (2010) On distance-based inconsistency reduction algorithms for pairwise comparisons. Logic J IGPL 18(6):859–869

Labib AW (2011) A supplier selection model: a comparison of fuzzy logic and the analytic hierarchy process. Int J Prod Res 49(21):6287–6299

Lee JW, Kim SH (2000) Using analytic network process and goal programming for interdependent information system project selection. Comput Oper Res 27(4):367–382

Levy J, Taji K (2007) Group decision support for hazards planning and emergency management: a group analytic network process (GANP) approach. Math Comput Model 46(7–8):906–917

Li T-S, Huang H-H (2009) Applying TRIZ and Fuzzy AHP to develop innovative design for automated manufacturing systems. Expert Syst Appl 36:8302–8312

Li S, Li JZ (2009) Hybridising human judgment, AHP, simulation and a fuzzy expert system for strategy formulation under uncertainty. Expert Syst Appl 36:5557–5564

Li H, Ma L (2007) Detecting and adjusting ordinal and cardinal inconsistencies through a graphical and optimal approach in ahp models. Comput Oper Res 34(3):780–798

Lin C (2007) A revised framework for deriving preference values from pairwise comparison matrices. Eur J Oper Res 176(2):1145–1150

Liu W (1999) A new method of rectifying judgment matrix. Syst Eng Theory Pract 6:30–34, in Chinese

Lootsma FA (1988) Numerical scaling of human judgment in pairwise-comparison methods for fuzzy multi-criteria decision analysis. In: Lootsma FA (ed) Mathematical models for decision support, vol 48, NATO ASI series F, computer and system sciences. Springer, Berlin, pp 57–88

Lootsma FA (1991) Scale sensitivity and rank preservation in a multiplicative variant of the AHP and SMART. Report 91-67, Faculty of Technical Mathematics and Informatics, Delft University of Technology, Delft

Lu ST, Lin CW, Ko PH (2007) Application of analytic network process (ANP) in assessing construction risk of urban bridge project. In: International conference on innovative computing, information and control (ICICIC 07), pp 169–169

Mikhailov L, Singh MG (2003) Fuzzy analytic network process and its application to the development of decision support systems. IEEE Trans Syst Man Cybern C Appl Rev 33(1):33–41

Moreno Jiménez JM, Vargas LG (1993) A probabilistic study of preference structures in the analytic hierarchy process with interval judgements. Math Comput Model 17(4/5):73–81

Niemira MP, Saaty TL (2004) An analytic network process model for financial-crisis forecasting. Int J Forecast 20(4):573–587

Pelaez JI, Lamata MT (2003) A new measure of consistency for positive reciprocal matrices. Comput Math Appl 46(12):1839–1845

Peng Y, Kou G, Wang G, Wu W, Shi Y (2011a) Ensemble of software defect predictors: an AHP-based evaluation method. Int J Inf Technol Decis Mak 10(1):187–206

Raisinghani MS, Meade L, Schkade LL (2007) Strategic e-business decision analysis using the analytic network process. Eng Manage IEEE Trans 54(4):673–686

Saaty TL (1977) A scaling method for priorities in hierarchical structures. J Math Psychol 15(3):234–281

Saaty TL (1978) Modeling unstructured decision problems-the theory of analytical hierarchies. Math Comput Simulat 20:147–158

Saaty TL (1979) Applications of analytical hierarchies. Math Comput Simulat 21:1–20

Saaty TL (1980) The analytical hierarchy process. McGraw-Hill, New York

Saaty TL (1986) Axiomatic foundation of the analytic hierarchy process. Manage Sci 32(7):841–855

Saaty RW (1987) The analytic hierarchy process – what it is and how it is used. Math Model 9(3–5):161–176

Saaty TL (1990) How to make a decision: the analytic hierarchy process. Eur J Oper Res 48(1):9–26

Saaty TL (1991) Some mathematical concepts of the analytic hierarchy process. Behaviormetrika 29:1–9

Saaty TL (1994) How to make a decision: the analytic hierarchy process. Interfaces 24:19–43

Saaty TL (1996) Decision making with dependence and feedback: the analytic network process. RWS Publications, Pittsburgh. ISBN 0-9620317-9-8

Saaty TL (1999) Fundamentals of the analytic network process. In: ISAHP 1999, Kobe, Japan, 12–14 Aug 1999

Saaty TL (2001a) Decision making with the analytic network process (ANP) and its "super deci-sions" software: the national missile defense (NMD) example. In: ISAHP 2001 proceedings, Bern, Switzerland, 2–4 Aug 2001

Saaty TL (2001b) Deriving the AHP 1–9 scale from first principles. In: ISAHP 2001 proceedings, Bern, Switzerland

Saaty TL (2003) Decision-making with the AHP: why is the principal eigenvector necessary. Eur J Oper Res 145(1):85–89

Saaty TL (2004) Fundamentals of the analytic network process: dependence and feedback in decision-making with a single network. J Syst Sci Syst Eng, published at Tsinghua University, Beijing, vol 13, no. 2, pp 129–157

Saaty TL (2005) Theory and applications of the analytic network process: decision making with benefits, opportunities, costs and risks. RWS Publications, Pittsburgh. ISBN 1-888603-06-2

Saaty TL (2006) Rank from comparisons and from ratings in the analytic hierarchy/network processes. Eur J Oper Res 168:557–570

Saaty TL (2008) The analytic network process. Iran J Oper Res 1(1):1–27

Saaty TL, Zoffer HJ (2011) Negotiating the Israeli-Palestinian controversy from a new perspective. Int J Inf Technol Decis Mak 10(1):5–64

Thurstone L (1927) A law of comparative judgment. Psychol Rev 34(4):273–286

Triantaphyllou E, Mann SH (1995) Using the analytic hierarchy process for decision making in engineering applications: Some challenges. Int J Ind Eng Appl Pract 2(1):35–44

Vargas LG (2008) The consistency index in reciprocal matrices: comparison of determinestic and statistical approaches. Eur J Oper Res 191:454–463

Wei CP, Zhang ZM (2000) An algorithm to improve the consistency of a comparison matrix. Syst Eng Theory Pract 8:62–66, in Chinese

Wu WW (2008) Choosing knowledge management strategies by using a combined ANP and DEMATEL approach. Expert Syst Appl 35(3):828–835

Xu Z, Wei C (1999) A consistency improving method in the analytic hierarchy process. Eur J Oper Res 116:443–449

Chapter 2
A New Consistency Test Index for the Data in the AHP/ANP

The consistency test is one of the critical components both in AHP and ANP. Currently, the consistency ratio (CR) proposed by Saaty is popularly used to test the consistencies of the pairwise comparison matrices. However, when the number of comparison matrices increases, the consistency test of comparison matrices both in the AHP and ANP becomes complicated. In an attempt to simplify the consistency test, Ergu et al. (2011a) proposed a maximum eigenvalue threshold as the new consistency index for the data in the AHP and ANP, which is mathematically equivalent to the CR method. In addition, a block diagonal matrix is introduced for the comparison matrices in the AHP/ANP to conduct consistency tests simultaneously. In this Chapter, the proposed new consistency test index is comprehensively described.

2.1 Basics of the AHP/ANP

2.1.1 The Positive Reciprocal Pairwise Comparison Matrix

The pairwise comparison technique, originally proposed by Thurstone (1927) is a well-established technique and widely used in analytical hierarchy process (AHP)/analytical network process (ANP) (Saaty 1980, 1994, 2008) to pairwise compare two attributes or alternatives with respect to a given criterion. All pair-wise comparisons are then arranged in a matrix $A = (a_{ij})_{n \times n}$, and popularly called pair-wise comparison matrix (PCM) or positive reciprocal matrix in literature, which has the following definitions and notations.

G. Kou et al., *Data Processing for the AHP/ANP*, Quantitative Management 1,
DOI 10.1007/978-3-642-29213-2_2, © Springer-Verlag Berlin Heidelberg 2013

Table 2.1 The average random index

n	1	2	3	4	5	6	7	8	9	10
RI	0	0	0.52	0.89	1.11	1.25	1.35	1.4	1.45	1.49

$$A = \begin{bmatrix} a_{11} & a_{12} & \cdots & a_{1n} \\ a_{21} & a_{22} & \cdots & a_{2n} \\ \vdots & \vdots & \ddots & \vdots \\ a_{n1} & a_{n2} & \cdots & a_{nn} \end{bmatrix}$$

Definition 2.1. A comparison matrix A is positive reciprocal matrix if $a_{ii} = 1$, $a_{ij} > 0$ and $a_{ij} = \frac{1}{a_{ji}}$ for all positive integer i and j.

Definition 2.2. A positive reciprocal matrix is perfectly consistent if $a_{ik}a_{kj} = a_{ij}$ for all i, j and k.

Definition 2.3. A positive reciprocal matrix is approximately consistent if $a_{ik}a_{kj} \approx a_{ij}$ for all i, j and k, where '$\approx$' denotes approximately or close to.

Definition 2.4. A positive reciprocal matrix is transitive if $A > C$ can be derived from $A > B$ and $B > C$ logically.

Definition 2.5. The pairwise comparison matrix can pass the consistency test, if the Consistency Ratio $CR = \frac{CI}{RI} < 0.1$, where the Consistency Index $CI = \frac{\lambda_{\max} - n}{n-1}$, RI is the average Random Index based on Matrix Size as shown in Table 2.1, $\lambda_{\max}$ is the maximum eigenvalue of matrix A, and n is the order of matrix A (Saaty 1991).

The pairwise comparison matrix (PCM) is composed of elements expressed on a numerical scale and the values of elements are given by decision makers based on their experiences and expertise in order to transform the qualitative attribute or criteria into measurable numbers. Saaty (1978, 2001b) suggested a 1–9 fundamental scale to compare two elements with respect to the criteria, and $n(n-1)/2$ comparisons are needed to complete a comparison matrix.

Once a set of pairwise comparison matrices are constructed for a decision problem, the priority weights of alternatives need to be derived from these matrices, and then a decision can be made in terms of the ranking order of the alternatives. Currently, there are more than 20 different methods that can be used to derive the priority weights of alternatives from a PCM, including the Normalization of the Column Sum Method and Arithmetic Mean of Normalized Columns Method (Saaty 1980), the Eigenvector Method (EM) (Saaty 2003), the Direct Least Squares Method (DLSM) and the Weighted Least Squares Method (WLSM) (Chu et al. 1979), the Logarithmic Least Squares Method (LLSM) (Crawford and Williams 1985)/Geometric Means Solution (Barzilai 1997), and the Logarithmic Goal Programming Method (GPM) (Bryson 1995) etc. Among these methods, the Eigenvector Method (EM) is used in *AHP Expert Choice Software*. In addition, the pairwise comparison matrix is the critical component in AHP/ANP, therefore, the basics of the AHP/ANP are briefly described below.

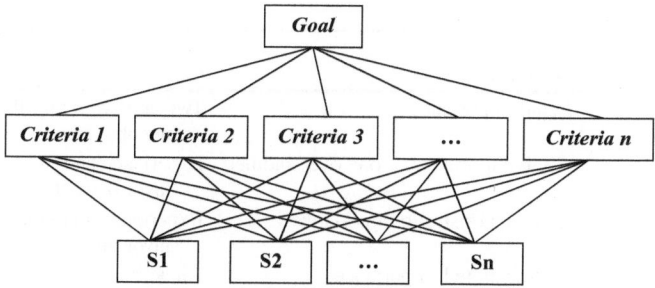

Fig. 2.1 The typical hierarchy structure with three levels in the AHP

2.1.2 Basics of the AHP

Analytic Hierarchy Process (AHP), initially proposed by Saaty in the 1970s (Saaty 1979, 1980), is one of the widely used multi-criteria decision making (MCDM) methods, and has been successfully applied to many practical decision making problems. In the AHP, a complicated decision problem can be decomposed into several hierarchies according to the related attributes or criteria. The typical AHP hierarchy structure with three levels is shown in Fig. 2.1.

When AHP is used to make a decision, first, a decision problem should be determined, then we need to decompose the decision into hierarchical structure showing the relationships of the goal, criteria and alternatives from the top to the bottom, corresponding to the first level, second level and third levels as shown in Fig. 2.1. The typical steps of AHP include the following five steps:

1. Define the problem and decompose the problem.
2. Construct a set of pairwise comparison matrices.
3. Calculate eigenvalues and eigenvectors by Eigenvector Method (EM).
4. Test the consistency of all comparison matrices.
5. Aggregate the final priorities of alternatives to make decision.

In the first step, a decision problem should be defined, then structure the decision hierarchically by breaking down the decision problem into a hierarchy of interrelated decision elements, which usually includes three hierarchy levels: objective level, criteria level and alternatives level. In the AHP, it is assumed that the relation of higher level elements from lower level elements is independent and the elements within a level are also assumed to be independent.

In the second step, elements within same level are pairwise compared with respect to a given criterion, which is located at higher level. The intangible attributes are measured by a scale of absolute judgments that represents how much one element more dominates another with respect to a given attribute. In AHP, Saaty (1978) proposed a 9-point integer scale as shown in Table 2.2 to quantify the intangible attributes or criteria into measurable numerical numbers. Then all pairwise comparisons are arranged in a pairwise comparison matrix A, as explained in Sect. 2.1.1.

Table 2.2 The Saaty's 9-points rating scale

Intensity of importance	Definition	Explanation
1	Equal importance	Two activities contribute equally to the objective
3	Weak importance of one over another	Experience and judgment slightly favor one activity over another
5	Essential or strong importance	Experience and judgment strongly favor one activity over another
7	Demonstrated importance	An activity is strongly favored and its dominance demonstrated in practice
9	Absolute importance	The evidence favoring one activity over another is of the highest possible order of affirmation
2,4,6,8	Intermediate values between the two adjacent judgments	When compromise is needed
Reciprocals of above nonzero	If activity i has one of the above nonzero numbers assigned to it when compared with activity j, then j has the reciprocal value when compared with i.	

In the third step, as stated previously, there are more than 20 prioritization methods that can be used to calculate the priority vectors, however, the Eigenvector Method (EM) introduced by Saaty is the most popular one, which has been embedded in *AHP Expert Choice Software and ANP SuperDecision Software.*

In the fourth step, the consistency of all comparison matrices should be tested before they are used to make decision. The popular method for testing consistency is consistency ratio (CR) proposed by Saaty, details will be given in Sect. 2.2.

In the final step, the priority vectors calculated from comparison matrices in each level are used to weigh the priorities in the next level. Repeat this process for every element, then synthesize all priorities of criteria and alternatives until the final priorities of the alternatives in the bottom level are obtained. For more details of AHP, the reader is referred to Saaty (1980, 1990, 1991, 1994).

2.1.3   Basics of the ANP

As reviewed previously, AHP has two assumptions (Saaty 1994): the independence of higher level elements from lower level elements and the independence of the elements within a level. These two assumptions simplify the calculations when analyzing multiple criteria decision making (MCDM) with quantitative and qualitative attributes. However, many decision problems can not be structured hierarchically due to the complexity and dynamics nature of decision problems. Therefore, the interaction of higher level elements with lower level elements and their dependence

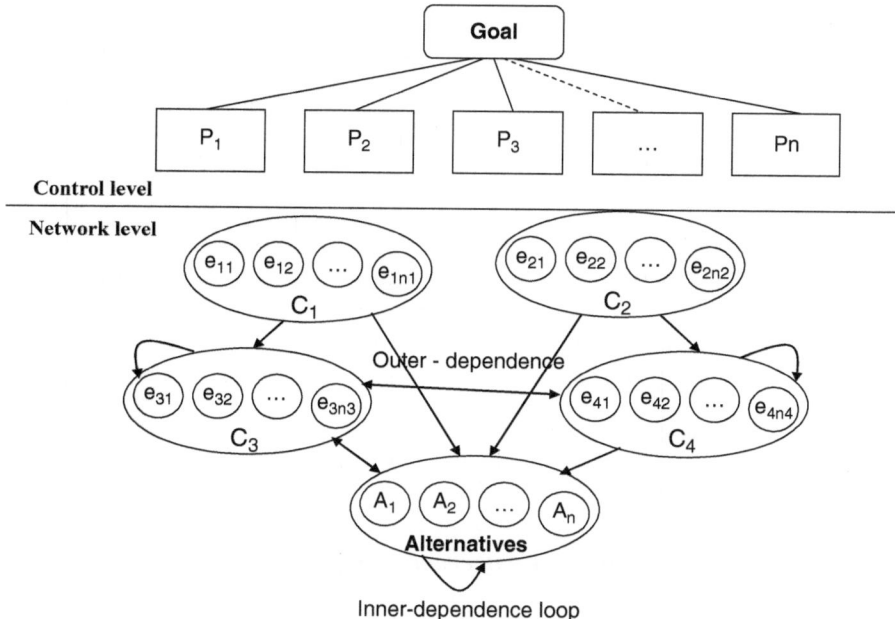

Fig. 2.2 The structure of ANP

should not be neglected. To address these inherent weaknesses in AHP, Saaty (1996) proposed the ANP for problems which cannot be structured hierarchically. The ANP, a generalization of the AHP, is capable of tackling sophisticated issue of dependence and feedback in a decision system, and provides a general framework to deal with decisions without making the above assumptions.

The ANP process has two parts, as shown in Fig. 2.2. The first part is a control hierarchy or network of criteria and subcriteria that controls the interactions. The second part consists of a network of influences among the elements and clusters (Saaty 1996). In ANP, there are outer-dependence and/or inner-dependence between the elements and clusters. The priority vectors in ANP are derived from pairwise comparison matrices and supermatrix is composed of elements which could also be matrices of column priorities, as shown in Fig. 2.3. Each of these supermatrices is weighed by the priority of its control criterion and the results are synthesized through addition for all the control criteria (Saaty 2005).

The main steps of the ANP include: (1) identify the elements and clusters; (2) create the model; (3) determine the interdependencies; (4) construct pairwise comparison matrices between the clusters and elements; (5) build supermatrix and solve the limit supermatrix. For more details of ANP, the reader is referred to Saaty (1996, 1999, 2001a, 2008).

$$
W =
\begin{array}{c}
\\
\\
C_1 \\
\\
\\
\\
C_2 \\
\\
\\
\\
C_N
\end{array}
\begin{array}{c}
\\
e_{11} \\
e_{12} \\
\vdots \\
e_{1n_1} \\
e_{21} \\
e_{22} \\
\vdots \\
e_{2n_2} \\
\vdots \\
e_{N1} \\
e_{N2} \\
\vdots \\
c_{N_i N}
\end{array}
\overset{
\begin{array}{ccc}
C_1 & C_2 & C_N \\
e_{11}\,e_{12}\cdots e_{1n_1} & e_{21}\,e_{22}\cdots e_{2n_2} & e_{N1}e_{N2}\cdots e_{Nn_N}
\end{array}
}{
\left[
\begin{array}{cccc}
W_{11} & W_{12} & \cdots & W_{1N} \\
W_{21} & W_{22} & & W_{2N} \\
\vdots & \vdots & & \vdots \\
W_{N1} & W_{N2} & & W_{NN}
\end{array}
\right]
}
$$

$$W_{ij} \quad \textit{Component of Supermatrix}$$

$$
W_{ij} =
\begin{bmatrix}
W_{i1}^{(j_1)} & W_{i1}^{(j_2)} & \cdots & W_{i1}^{(j_{n_j})} \\
W_{i2}^{(j_1)} & W_{i2}^{(j_2)} & \cdots & W_{i2}^{(j_{n_j})} \\
\vdots & \vdots & & \vdots \\
W_{in_i}^{(j_1)} & W_{in_i}^{(j_2)} & \cdots & W_{in_i}^{(j_{n_j})}
\end{bmatrix}
$$

Fig. 2.3 The supermatrix of a network

2.2   Consistency Test Issue in the AHP/ANP

2.2.1   Analysis of the Consistency Ratio (CR) Method

During the process of making decisions, there will be inconsistency issue occurring when comparing different attributes or criteria as the decision problems are complicated in nature. For instance, suppose attribute A is 2 times important as attribute B, and attribute B is 3 times important as attribute C, however, attribute A is only 4 times important as attribute C instead of 6 times. Likewise, the values of A is bigger than B, B is bigger than C, however C is bigger than A, namely, $A > B$, $B > C$, but $C > A$. Both of these issues are called inconsistency (Saaty 1991). Therefore, the consistency test is necessary for comparison matrix before the priority vectors of the comparison matrix can be calculated. If the consistency test for the comparison matrix is failed, the inconsistent elements in the comparison matrix has to be revised, otherwise, the result of decision analysis process is meaningless.

The most widely used consistency index is the consistency ratio (CR) (Saaty 1991), that is,

$$CR = \frac{CI}{RI} < 0.1 \tag{2.1}$$

where $CI = \frac{\lambda_{\max}-n}{n-1}$ is the consistency index, RI is the average random index based on Matrix Size shown in Table 2.1, $\lambda_{\max}$ is the maximum eigenvalue of matrix A, and n is the order of matrix A.

According to rule of thumb, the comparison matrix is consistent only if the value of CR is less than 0.1. The consistency test includes the following four steps:

Step 1: Calculate the $\lambda_{\max}$ of one comparison matrix.
Step 2: Calculate the value of CI using the formula $CI = \frac{\lambda_{\max}-n}{n-1}$.
Step 3: Calculate the CR using the formula $CR = \frac{CI}{RI}$ and Table 2.1.
Step 4: Compare the value of CR with the consistency threshold 0.1 to judge whether the comparison is consistent.

There is a major shortcoming when using CR as the consistency index for comparison matrices, as above steps has to be calculated repeatedly for each comparison matrix to test the consistency.

2.2.2 The Issues of Consistency Test in the AHP/ANP

The AHP is the special case of ANP while ANP is an extensive and complementary method of the AHP. Therefore, in the following, we mainly focus on the consistency issue in the ANP. Similar to the AHP, the consistency of each comparison matrices in ANP needs to be tested using the CR method. If the comparison matrices pass the consistency test, then the priorities derived from the comparison matrices are added as parts of the columns of the supermatrix of a network (Saaty 2008), which is shown in Fig. 2.3. Otherwise, this comparison matrix has to be revised by experts.

Therefore, the consistency test will be much more complicated in the ANP than in the AHP since, in the ANP, there exist more comparison matrices derived from the supermatrix of a network as shown in Fig. 2.3.

In Fig. 2.3, each judgment indicates the dominance of an element in the column on the left over an element in the row on the top. Assume $W_{ij} \neq 0$ for all $1 \leq i, j \leq N$, both inner-clusters and outer-clusters have interactions. In above supermatrix, there are two kinds of comparison matrices in the ANP, the inner-clusters comparison matrices and the outer-clusters comparison matrices. From the C_1 cluster to the C_N cluster, the number of the comparison matrices in the inner-cluster is n_1 with order n_1, n_2 with order n_2, $\ldots$, and n_N with order n_N respectively. The number of the comparison matrices in the outer-cluster includes: $(N-1)\,n_1$ with orders $n_2, n_3, \ldots, n_N$; $(N-1)\,n_2$ with orders $n_1, n_3, \ldots, n_N$; $(N-1)\,n_3$ with orders $n_1, n_2, n_4, \ldots, n_N$; $\ldots$; $(N-1)\,n_N$ with orders $n_1, n_2, n_3, \ldots, n_{N-1}$.

Inner-cluster comparison matrices
in the ANP

Quantity	Matrices order
n_1	$n_1 \times n_1$
n_2	$n_2 \times n_2$
$\vdots$	$\vdots$
n_N	$n_N \times n_N$

The total number of Inner-cluster comparison matrices is $n_1 + n_2 + \cdots + n_N$.

Outer-cluster comparison matrices in the ANP

Quantity	Matrices order
$(N-1)\,n_1$	$n_2 \times n_2, n_3 \times n_3, \ldots, n_N \times n_N$
$(N-1)\,n_2$	$n_1 \times n_1, n_3 \times n_3, \ldots, n_N \times n_N$
$\vdots$	$\vdots$
$(N-1)\,n_N$	$n_1 \times n_1, n_3 \times n_3, \ldots, n_{N-1} \times n_{N-1}$

The total number of Outer-cluster comparison matrices is $(N-1)\,(n_1 + n_2 + \cdots + n_N)$.

Therefore, the total number of all the comparison matrices in the ANP is $N(n_1 + n_2 + \cdots + n_N)$. Hence, the CR method has to be calculated the CRs $N\,(n_1 + n_2 + \cdots + n_N)$ times for all comparison matrices.

To sum up:

1. The consistency ratio is calculated repeatedly for each comparison matrix in the CR method.
2. The CRs of the comparison matrices in the ANP need to be calculated $4N(n_1 + n_2 + \cdots + n_N)$ times since the total number of the comparison matrices is $N(n_1 + n_2 + \cdots + n_N)$ from C_1 cluster to C_N cluster which contain n_1 elements to n_N elements respectively.

Therefore, the traditional CR method is very complicated in practice, especially for the ANP. In the following, a new consistency index, called Maximum eigenvalue threshold, is proposed to test the consistency of the comparison matrices in AHP/ANP. Details are followed next.

2.3   The New Consistency Index: Maximum Eigenvalue Threshold for the AHP/ANP

In the formula $CR = (\lambda_{\max} - n)\,/\,(n-1)\,RI$, the CR is only dominated by the $\lambda_{\max}$ for the comparison matrices in the same order, which are commonly occurred in the ANP. Therefore, we can derive the following corollary.

Table 2.3 The threshold $\lambda^n_{max\,thrd}$ of the maximum eigenvalue and the corresponding RI

n	1	2	3	4	5	6	7	8	9	10
RI	0	0	0.52	0.89	1.11	1.25	1.35	1.4	1.45	1.49
$\lambda^n_{max\,thrd}$	1	2	3.104	4.267	5.444	6.781	7.81	8.98	10.16	11.341

Corollary 2.1. *The inequality* $CR < 0.1$ *is mathematically equivalent to the inequality* $\lambda_{max} < \lambda^n_{max\,threshold}$ *or* $\Delta\lambda_{max} < 0$, *where* λ_{max} *denotes the maximum eigenvalue of the comparison matrix with order n,* $\lambda^n_{max\,threshold}$ *represents the corresponding maximum eigenvalue threshold with order n, which is listed in Table 2.3,* $\Delta\lambda_{max}$ *denotes the bias between the maximum eigenvalue and its corresponding threshold. The proofs can be done as the following:*

Proof. If

$$CR = \frac{CI}{RI} = \frac{\lambda_{max} - n}{(n-1)\,RI} < 0.1 \tag{2.2}$$

That is

$$CR = \frac{CI}{RI} < 0.1 \Leftrightarrow CI < 0.1RI \tag{2.3}$$

$$\Leftrightarrow \frac{\lambda_{max} - n}{n-1} < 0.1RI \tag{2.4}$$

$$\Leftrightarrow \lambda_{max} - n < 0.1RI(n-1) \tag{2.5}$$

$$\Leftrightarrow \lambda_{max} < 0.1RI(n-1) + n \tag{2.6}$$

where the symbol "$\Leftrightarrow$" denotes equivalence. Let the right value be the maximum eigenvalue threshold $\lambda^n_{max\,threshold}$ (in short $\lambda^n_{max\,thrd}$), namely,

$$\lambda^n_{max\,thrd} = 0.1RI(n-1) + n \tag{2.7}$$

Therefore

$$CR < 0.1 \Leftrightarrow \lambda_{max} < \lambda^n_{max\,thrd} \tag{2.8}$$

$$\Leftrightarrow \nabla\lambda_{max} = \lambda_{max} - \lambda^n_{max\,thrd} < 0 \tag{2.9}$$

$\square$

Since the CR method is mathematically equivalent to the maximum eigenvalue threshold method, the corresponding maximum eigenvalue threshold $\lambda^n_{max\,thrd}$ of the comparison matrices with order n can be easily calculated using the formula (2.7) and the corresponding value of RI in Table 2.1. The results are listed in Table 2.3.

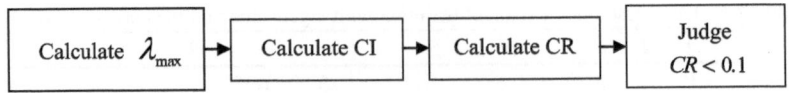

Fig. 2.4 The calculation processes of the *CR* method

From the Table 2.3, once the maximum eigenvalue $\lambda_{\max}$ of a comparison matrix is calculated, the consistency of this comparison matrix can be tested by comparing the $\lambda_{\max}$ with the maximum eigenvalue threshold $\lambda^n_{\max\,thrd}$ without calculating the CI and CR. For instance, assume $\lambda_{\max} = 5.2$ for a comparison matrix of order 5, the comparison matrix is consistent because the $\lambda_{\max} = 5.2 < \lambda^5_{\max\,thrd} = 5.444$, which is equivalent to $CR = 0.045 < 0.1$. Therefore, the maximum eigenvalue threshold $\lambda^n_{\max\,thrd}$ can be used as a new consistency index for the ANP to test whether a comparison matrix is consistent. The specific principle of consistency test can be defined as follows:

Consistency test principle: If $\lambda^i_{\max} < \lambda^n_{\max\,thrd}$, that is, $\Delta\lambda^i_{\max} < 0$, the ith comparison matrix passes the consistency test. If $\lambda^i_{\max} \geq \lambda^n_{\max\,thrd}$, that is, $\Delta\lambda^i_{\max} \geq 0$, the ith comparison matrix fails the consistency test. The ith comparison matrix should be revised.

2.3.1 The Advantages of Maximum Eigenvalue Threshold for AHP/ANP

The CR method is the most widely used consistency test method in the AHP/ANP. Although it is proved that the CR method developed by Saaty is mathematically equivalent to the $\lambda^n_{\max\,thrd}$ method, that is, $CR = \frac{CI}{RI} < 0.1$ is equivalent to $\lambda^n_{\max} < \lambda^n_{\max\,thrd}$ or $\Delta\lambda^n_{\max} < 0$, the maximum threshold $\lambda^n_{\max\,thrd}$ method is easier to implement than the *CR* method.

The principles of consistency test of the *CR* method and the $\lambda^n_{\max\,thrd}$ method are shown in inequalities (2.10) and (2.11) respectively:

$$CR = \frac{CI}{RI} = \frac{\lambda_{\max} - n}{(n-1)\,RI} < 0.1 \tag{2.10}$$

$$\lambda_{\max} < \lambda^n_{\max\,thrd} \quad \text{Or} \quad \Delta\lambda^n_{\max} < 0 \tag{2.11}$$

The detailed processes of the *CR* method and the $\lambda^n_{\max\,thrd}$ method are shown in the Figs. 2.4 and 2.5.

Clearly, compared to the CR method, in $\lambda^n_{\max\,thrd}$ method, there is no need to calculate the two middle steps as shown in Fig. 2.4, which saves $2N(n_1 + n_2 + \cdots + n_N)$ times in calculation. Therefore, the advantages of the $\lambda^n_{\max\,thrd}$ method can be summarized into two aspects: efficient and easier to be implemented.

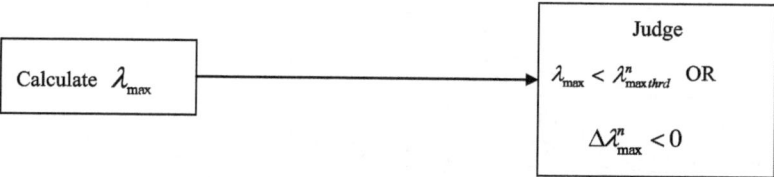

Fig. 2.5 The calculation processes of the $\lambda^n_{max\ thrd}$ method

Fig. 2.6 The typical hierarchy structure with three levels in the AHP

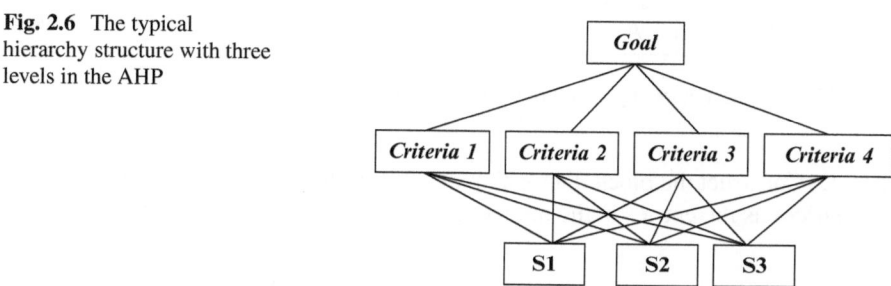

2.4 The Processes of Data Consistency Test in AHP/ANP

The principle of consistency test by maximum eigenvalue threshold method has been proposed in Sect. 2.3. For a pairwise comparison matrix (PCM), only two steps are needed to test whether the PCM passes the consistency test: (1) calculate the maximum eigenvalue λ_{max} and (2) compare it with the maximum eigenvalue threshold as shown in Table 2.3. If $\lambda_{max} < \lambda_{max\ thrd}$ or $\Delta\lambda_{max} < 0$, then the PCM passes the consistency test, otherwise, the inconsistent elements should be identified and adjusted until it satisfies the consistency test.

To further simplify the processes of the consistency test in the AHP/ANP, in Ergu et al. (2011d), the block diagonal matrix, based on the comparison matrices in the same level or different levels, was proposed to test the consistencies of several comparison matrices simultaneously. Details will be presented below. As the AHP is a special case in the ANP, without losing generality, two typical cases of AHP structures with three levels and four levels respectively are used to illustrate the block diagonal matrix and the consistency test methodologies.

Case-1: the block diagonal matrix is constructed for a typical AHP model with three levels as shown in Fig. 2.6.

In this hierarchy structure, there are five comparison matrices: One with order four for the criteria with respect to the goal in the first level, denoted as A, and four with order three for the three alternatives with respect to the four criteria in the second level, denoted as $C1$, $C2$, $C3$ and $C4$. The consistency test for the comparison matrix A can be tested independently, while the other four comparison matrices with the same order can be tested simultaneously. The consistency test includes three steps:

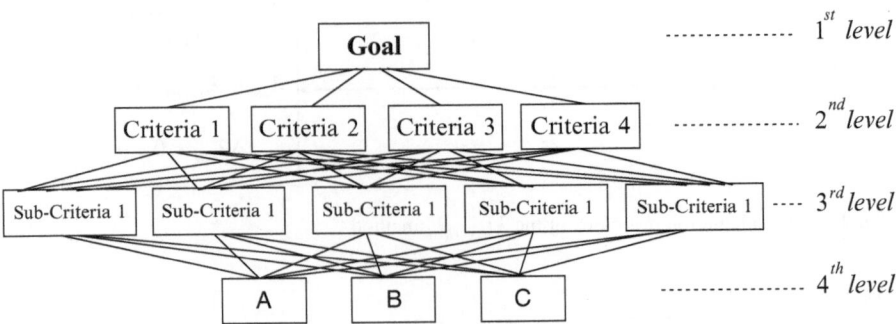

Fig. 2.7 The typical hierarchy structure with four levels in the AHP

Step 1: Construct the block diagonal matrix (B in short) using the five comparison matrices as the entries in the main diagonal:

$$B = \begin{pmatrix} A & & & & \\ & C1 & & & \\ & & C2 & & \\ & & & C3 & \\ & & & & C4 \end{pmatrix} \tag{2.12}$$

Step 2: Calculate the eigenvalues in the block diagonal matrix B. According to the notations of the block diagonal matrix, the maximum eigenvalues in the block diagonal matrix are the corresponding maximum eigenvalues of the comparison matrices A, $C1$, $C2$, $C3$ and $C4$ respectively, which are denoted as $\lambda^i{}_{max}$ ($i = 0, 1, 2, 3, 4$).

Step 3: Calculate the maximum eigenvalue bias $\Delta\lambda^i_{max}$ ($i = 0, 1, 2, 3, 4$) using the following formulas, and judge its consistency using the corresponding condition mentioned above.

$$\Delta\lambda^0_{max} = \lambda^0_{max} - \lambda^4_{max\,thrd} \tag{2.13}$$

$$\Delta\lambda^i_{max} = \left(\lambda^1_{max}\,\lambda^2_{max}\,\lambda^3_{max}\,\lambda^4_{max}\right) - \lambda^3_{max\,thrd} \tag{2.14}$$

If $\Delta\lambda^i_{max} < 0$ ($i = 0, 1, 2, 3, 4$), then the ith comparison matrix passes the consistency test, otherwise, it fails the consistency test. For instance, assume $\Delta\lambda^2_{max} < 0$ and $\Delta\lambda^4_{max} > 0$, the comparison matrix $C2$ passes the consistency test and is consistent while the comparison matrix $C4$ failed the consistency test, and its elements should be revised.

Case-2: the block diagonal matrix is constructed for a typical AHP structure with four levels as shown in Fig. 2.7.

In this four-level structure, there are ten pairwise comparison matrices.

In the 1st level: One matrix with order four with respect to the Goal, denoted as G.

In the 2nd level: Four comparison matrices with order five for the five Sub-Criteria with respect to all four criteria, denoted as $C1, C2, C3$ and $C4$.

In the 3rd level: Five comparison matrices for the three Alternatives with respect to all the five Sub-Criteria, denoted as S1, S2, S3, S4 and S5 respectively.

After calculating each λ^i_{max} $(i = 0, 1, 2, \cdots, 9)$ for the ten comparison matrices, one has to calculate the CR ten times for ten comparison matrices before judging whether the CR is less than 0.1. The complicities of CR calculation will be increased with the increase of the comparison matrices in the ANP. However, if the proposed maximum eigenvalue threshold index is used to test each consistency issue for ten comparison matrices, all the inconsistencies can be tested by using the maximum eigenvalue threshold method, $\lambda^i_{max} < \lambda^n_{max\,thrd}$. For instance, comparing the λ^0_{max} with the threshold $\lambda^4_{lim\,max}$ for the first comparison matrix in order four, comparing the λ^i_{max} $(i = 1, \cdots, 4)$ with the threshold $\lambda^5_{max\,thrd}$ for the second four comparison matrices in order five, and comparing the λ^i_{max} $(i = 5, \cdots, 9)$ with the threshold $\lambda^3_{max\,thrd}$ for the last five comparison matrices in order three.

In above case, there are two basic principles of consistency test using the maximum eigenvalues, as shown below.

Basic Principle 1. Level-by-level test – Test the consistencies of the comparison matrices for each level. That is, test the consistencies of the comparison matrices with the same order in the same level one by one.

The processes of this method include the following steps.

Step 1: Construct the corresponding block diagonal matrix denoted as, B_1, B_2 and B_3 for the comparison matrices in each level using the corresponding comparison matrices as the entries in the main diagonals:

$$B_1 = G \tag{2.15}$$

$$B_2 = \begin{pmatrix} C1 & & & \\ & C2 & & \\ & & C3 & \\ & & & C4 \end{pmatrix} \tag{2.16}$$

$$B_3 = \begin{pmatrix} S1 & & & & \\ & S2 & & & \\ & & S3 & & \\ & & & S4 & \\ & & & & S5 \end{pmatrix} \tag{2.17}$$

Note: If the order of the block diagonal matrix is acceptable, then the block
   diagonal matrix B can be constructed by all comparison matrices in the whole
   level as the entries in the main diagonal to calculate the eigenvalues of all
   comparison matrices simultaneously.

$$B = \begin{pmatrix} G & & & & & & & & & \\ & C1 & & & & & & & & \\ & & C2 & & & & & & & \\ & & & C3 & & & & & & \\ & & & & C4 & & & & & \\ & & & & & S1 & & & & \\ & & & & & & S2 & & & \\ & & & & & & & S3 & & \\ & & & & & & & & S4 & \\ & & & & & & & & & S5 \end{pmatrix} \tag{2.18}$$

Step 2: Calculate the eigenvalues in the block diagonal matrix B_1, B_2 and B_3
   respectively. Or directly calculate the eigenvalues of the block diagonal matrix B.
   According to the notations of the block diagonal matrix, the maximum eigenvalues in the block diagonal matrix are the corresponding maximum eigenvalues
   of the comparison matrices G, $C1$, $C2$, $C3$, $C4$, $S1$, $S2$, $S3$, $S4$ and $S5$
   respectively, denoted as $\lambda^i{}_{max}(i = 0, 1, 2, 3, 4, 5, 6, 7, 8, 9)$.
Step 3: Calculate the maximum eigenvalue biases for the comparison matrices for
   each level using the following formulas, and judge its consistency using the
   corresponding condition mentioned above, that is, $\Delta\lambda^0_{max}$ for the first level,
   $\Delta\lambda^i_{max}$ ($i = 1, 2, 3, 4$) for the second level, $\Delta\lambda^i_{max}$ ($i = 5, 6, 7, 8, 9$) for the
   third level.

The 1st level : $\Delta\lambda^0_{max} = \lambda^0_{max} - \lambda^4_{max\,thrd}$ $\hspace{2cm}$ (2.19)

The 2nd level : $\Delta\lambda^i_{max} = \left(\lambda^1_{max}\ \lambda^2_{max}\ \lambda^3_{max}\ \lambda^4_{max}\right) - \lambda^5_{max\,thrd}$ $\hspace{1cm}$ (2.20)

The 3rd level : $\Delta\lambda^i_{max} = \left(\lambda^5_{max}\ \lambda^6_{max}\ \lambda^7_{max}\ \lambda^8_{max}\ \lambda^9_{max}\right) - \lambda^3_{max\,thrd}$ $\hspace{0.5cm}$ (2.21)

If $\Delta\lambda^i_{max} < 0$ ($i = 0, 1, 2, 3, 4, 5, 6, 7, 8, 9$), then the ith comparison matrix
passes the consistency test, otherwise, it fails the consistency test. The specific
processes of consistency test are the same processes illustrated previously.

Basic Principle 2. Whole-level test – Test the whole consistencies of the comparison matrices simultaneously.

The processes of this method include:

Step 1: Construct the block diagonal matrix B using all the comparison matrices as the entries in the main diagonals at one time (simultaneously)

$$
B = \begin{pmatrix}
G \\
 & C1 \\
 & & C2 \\
 & & & C3 \\
 & & & & C4 \\
 & & & & & S1 \\
 & & & & & & S2 \\
 & & & & & & & S3 \\
 & & & & & & & & S4 \\
 & & & & & & & & & S5
\end{pmatrix} \tag{2.22}
$$

Step 2: Calculate the eigenvalues of the block diagonal matrix B. Then the maximum eigenvalues of the comparison matrices $G, C1, C2, C3, C4, S1, S2, S3, S4$ and $S5$ can be calculated, denoted as $\lambda^i{}_{\max}$ ($i = 0, 1, 2, 3, 4, 5, 6, 7, 8, 9$) respectively.

Step 3: Calculate the maximum eigenvalue biases for all comparison matrices using the following formula, and judge its consistency using the corresponding condition mentioned above.

$$
\Delta\lambda^i_{\max} = \left(\lambda^0_{\max} \quad \lambda^1_{\max} \quad \lambda^2_{\max} \quad \lambda^3_{\max} \quad \lambda^4_{\max} \quad \lambda^5_{\max} \quad \lambda^6_{\max} \quad \lambda^7_{\max} \quad \lambda^8_{\max} \quad \lambda^9_{\max}\right)
$$
$$
- \left(\lambda^4_{\max\,thrd} \quad \lambda^5_{\max\,thrd} \quad \lambda^5_{\max\,thrd} \quad \lambda^5_{\max\,thrd} \quad \lambda^5_{\max\,thrd} \quad \lambda^5_{\max\,thrd} \quad \lambda^3_{\max\,thrd} \quad \lambda^3_{\max\,thrd} \quad \lambda^3_{\max\,thrd} \quad \lambda^3_{\max\,thrd}\right)
$$
$$
\tag{2.23}
$$

Likewise, if $\Delta\lambda^i_{\max} < 0$ ($i = 0, 1, 2, 3, 4, 5, 6, 7, 8, 9$), then the ith comparison matrix passes the consistency test, otherwise, it fails the consistency test. The specific processes of consistency test are the same processes illustrated previously.

2.5 Illustrative Example

For simplicity, an example selecting the best computer system firstly introduced by Triantaphyllou and Mann (1995), which has the typical hierarchy structure as shown in Fig. 2.6, is used to illustrate *Basic Principle 1 – Level-by-level test* method. This example will again be used to illustrate *Basic Principle 2 – Whole-level test* method in *Example 7.3*. The five comparison matrices provided by Triantaphyllou and Mann are denoted as A, C1, C2, C3, and C4 respectively. Follow above three steps of *Basic Principle 1* to test the consistencies of five matrices:

Step 1: Construct the block diagonal matrix B showed below using the matrices A, C1, C2, C3 and C4.

Columns1through11   Columns12through16

1.0000	5.0000	3.0000	7.0000	0	0	0	0	0	0	0	0	0	0	0	0
0.2000	1.0000	0.3333	5.0000	0	0	0	0	0	0	0	0	0	0	0	0
0.3333	3.0000	1.0000	6.0000	0	0	0	0	0	0	0	0	0	0	0	0
0.1429	0.2000	0.1667	1.0000	0	0	0	0	0	0	0	0	0	0	0	0
0	0	0	0	1.0000	6.0000	8.0000	0	0	0	0	0	0	0	0	0
0	0	0	0	0.1667	1.0000	4.0000	0	0	0	0	0	0	0	0	0
0	0	0	0	0.1250	0.2500	1.0000	0	0	0	0	0	0	0	0	0
0	0	0	0	0	0	0	1.0000	7.0000	0.2000	0	0	0	0	0	0
0	0	0	0	0	0	0	0.1429	1.0000	0.1250	0	0	0	0	0	0
0	0	0	0	0	0	0	5.0000	8.0000	1.0000	0	0	0	0	0	0
0	0	0	0	0	0	0	0	0	0	1.0000	8.0000	6.0000	0	0	0
0	0	0	0	0	0	0	0	0	0	0.1250	1.0000	0.2500	0	0	0
0	0	0	0	0	0	0	0	0	0	0.1667	4.0000	1.0000	0	0	0
0	0	0	0	0	0	0	0	0	0	0	0	0	1.0000	5.0000	4.0000
0	0	0	0	0	0	0	0	0	0	0	0	0	0.2000	1.0000	0.3333
0	0	0	0	0	0	0	0	0	0	0	0	0	0.2500	3.0000	1.0000

Step 2: Calculate the eigenvalue of block diagonal matrix B, and obtain the maximum eigenvalues of the corresponding block diagonal sub-matrix A, C1, C2, C3 and C4. That is:

$$\lambda^0_{max} = 4.2365, \ \lambda^1_{max} = 3.1356, \ \lambda^2_{max} = 3.2470, \ \lambda^3_{max} = 3.1356, \ \lambda^4_{max} = 3.0858$$

Step 3: Test the consistency using the maximum eigenvalue threshold method. That is:

$$\Delta\lambda^0_{max} = \lambda^0_{max} - \lambda^4_{max\ thrd} = 4.2365 - 4.267 = -0.0305 < 0$$

The result shows that the comparison matrix A is consistent.

$$\Delta\lambda^i_{max} = \left(\lambda^1_{max}, \ \lambda^2_{max}, \ \lambda^3_{max}, \ \lambda^4_{max}\right) - \lambda^3_{max\ thrd}$$

$$= (3.1356, \ 3.2470, \ 3.1356, \ 3.0858) - 3.104$$

$$= (\ 0.0316, \ 0.143, \ 0.0316, -0.0182)$$

Obviously, only $\Delta\lambda^4_{max} < 0$, which means only the comparison matrix $C4$ is consistent, and others are inconsistent.

When the comparison matrix failed to the consistency test, there are three ways can be done (Saaty 2008): (1) Identify the most inconsistent judgment in the matrix, (2) Determine the range of values to which that judgment can be changed corresponding to which the inconsistency would be improved, (3) Ask the judge to change her/his judgment to be an acceptable value in that range.

Then, how to identify the most inconsistent judgment in the inconsistent matrix? There are many methods for improving the consistency ratio in literature. In Chap. 3, an induced bias matrix model (IBMM) is introduced to simply identify and adjust the most inconsistent elements in the inconsistent comparison matrix.

References

Barzilai J (1997) Deriving weights from pairwise comparison matrices. J Opl Res Soc 48:1226–1232

Bryson N (1995) A goal programming method for generating priority vectors. J Opl Res Soc 46:641–648

Chu A, Kalaba R, Springam K (1979) A comparison of two methods for determining the weights of belonging to fuzzy sets. J Opt Theory Appl 27:531–541

Crawford G, Williams C (1985) A note on the analysis of subjective judgment matrices. J Math Psychol 29:387–405

Ergu D, Kou G, Peng Y, Shi Y (2011a) A new consistency index for comparison matrices in the ANP, New State of MCDM in the 21st Century. Lecture notes in economics and mathematical systems, vol 648, part 1, pp 47–56

Ergu D, Kou G, Peng Y, Shi Y, Shi Yu (2011d) The analytic hierarchy process: task scheduling and resource allocation in cloud computing environment. J Supercomput. doi:10.1007/s11227-011-0625-1

Saaty TL (1978) Modeling unstructured decision problems-the theory of analytical hierarchies. Math Comput Simulat 20:147–158

Saaty TL (1979) Applications of analytical hierarchies. Math Comput Simulat 21:1–20

Saaty TL (1980) The analytical hierarchy process. McGraw-Hill, New York

Saaty TL (1990) How to make a decision: the analytic hierarchy process. Eur J Oper Res 48(1):9–26

Saaty TL (1991) Some mathematical concepts of the analytic hierarchy process. Behaviormetrika 29:1–9

Saaty TL (1994) How to make a decision: the analytic hierarchy process. Interfaces 24:19–43

Saaty TL (1996) Decision making with dependence and feedback: the analytic network process. RWS Publications, Pittsburgh. ISBN 0-9620317-9-8

Saaty TL (1999) Fundamentals of the analytic network process. In: ISAHP 1999, Kobe, Japan, 12–14 Aug 1999

Saaty TL (2001a) Decision making with the analytic network process (ANP) and its "super decisions" software: the national missile defense (NMD) example. In: ISAHP 2001 proceedings, Bern, Switzerland, 2–4 Aug 2001

Saaty TL (2001b) Deriving the AHP 1–9 scale from first principles. In: ISAHP 2001 proceedings, Bern, Switzerland

Saaty TL (2003) Decision-making with the AHP: why is the principal eigenvector necessary. Eur J Oper Res 145(1):85–89

Saaty TL (2005) Theory and applications of the analytic network process: decision making with benefits, opportunities, costs and risks. RWS Publications, Pittsburgh. ISBN 1-888603-06-2

Saaty TL (2008) The analytic network process. Iran J Oper Res 1(1):1–27

Thurstone L (1927) A law of comparative judgment. Psychol Rev 34(4):273–286

Triantaphyllou E, Mann SH (1995) Using the analytic hierarchy process for decision making in engineering applications: Some challenges. Int J Ind Eng Appl Pract 2(1):35–44

Chapter 3
IBMM for Inconsistent Data Identification and Adjustment in the AHP/ANP

As stated previously, the inconsistent elements should be identified if the pairwise comparison matrix (PCM) failed to the consistency test, therefore, the methods for identifying and adjusting the inconsistent elements in the PCM have been extensively studied since the AHP/ANP were developed by Saaty. However, existing methods are either too complicated to be applied in the revising process of the inconsistent comparison matrix or are difficult to preserve most of the original comparison information due to the use of a new pairwise comparison matrix. Therefore, Ergu et al. (2011b) developed a simple method for improving the consistency ratio of the pairwise comparison matrix in ANP, namely, an induced bias matrix (IBM) was developed to identify and adjust the inconsistent data in the ANP/AHP. The proposed method was further extended to estimate the missing item scores, optimize the questionnaire design and analyze the risk in decision making as well as task scheduling and resource allocation (Ergu et al. 2011c, 2011d, 2011e; Ergu and Kou 2011). To make the proposed model more comprehensive and robust, Ergu et al. (2011f) integrated the fundamental theorems and corollaries into one model, the induced bias matrix model (IBMM), and the related theorems and corollaries were also proved mathematically in Ergu et al. (2011b, 2011c). In this Chapter, all theorems and corollaries related to IBMM and their proofs are discussed systematically in order to understand the proposed IBMM explicitly.

3.1 The Theorems of Induced Bias Matrix Model (IBMM)

To efficiently identify the inconsistent elements and preserve most of the original pairwise comparison information, an induced bias matrix (IBM), which is only based on the original PCM, was proposed in Ergu et al. (2011b). In addition, the following *Theorem 3.1* was developed as the theorem of inconsistency identification method and *Corollary 3.1 and 3.2* were developed based on this theorem. The *Corollary 3.1* was proposed to estimate the uncertain or missing values in a PCM and proved mathematically in Ergu et al. (2011c). The *Corollary 3.2* shows that the farthest value should be identified as the inconsistent element from the induced bias matrix (IBM). Besides, the *Corollary 3.3* was further proposed to analyze the elements in the main diagonal of the IBM in Ergu et al. (2011c). All the theorem and corollaries are presented below.

Theorem 3.1. *The induced bias matrix $C = AA - nA$ should be a zero matrix if comparison matrix A is perfectly consistent.*

Corollary 3.1. *The induced bias matrix $C = AA - nA$ should be as close as possible to zero matrix if comparison matrix A is approximately consistent.*

Corollary 3.2. *There must be some inconsistent elements in induced bias matrix C deviating far away from zero if the pairwise matrix is inconsistent.*

Corollary 3.3. *Despite that the comparison matrix A is consistent or not, all entries in the main diagonal of the induced bias matrix $C = AA - nA$ should be zeroes giving that the comparison matrix A is satisfied with the reciprocal condition.*

The above mentioned theorem and corollaries can be integrated into one model, an induced bias matrix model (IBMM), which includes the following three theorems.

The Theorems of the Induced Bias Matrix Model (IBMM):

Theorem 3.2. *The induced bias matrix $C = AA - nA$ should be equal (or close) to a zero matrix if comparison matrix A is perfectly (or approximately) consistent. That is*

$$C = AA - nA \begin{cases} = 0 & if\ a_{ik}a_{kj} = a_{ij} \\ \approx 0 & if\ a_{ik}a_{kj} \approx a_{ij} \end{cases}$$

where A is the original PCM while a_{ij} represents the values of PCM. The "n" denotes the order of PCM.

Notes:

1. where A can be replaced with the block diagonal matrix consisting of several reciprocal pairwise comparison matrices to identify the inconsistent elements simultaneously.
2. where A can be replaced with the revised 'complete' PCM through replacing the missing values in the incomplete PCM with unknown variables $x,\ 1/x;y,\ 1/y;z,\ 1/z\ etc.$ to estimate the missing or uncertain values.

Theorem 3.3. *There must be some inconsistent elements in the induced bias matrix (IBM) C deviating far away from zero if the pairwise matrix is inconsistent. Especially, any row or column of matrix C contains at least one positive element.*

Theorem 3.4. *All entries in the main diagonal of the induced bias matrix (IBM)* $C = AA - nA$ *should be zeroes whether matrix A is consistent or not as long as the comparison matrix A satisfies the reciprocal condition.*

3.1.1   The Theoretical Proofs of IBMM

In the following, the above three theorems of induced bias matrix method are proved mathematically and demonstrated using some concrete illustrative examples.

Theorem 3.2. *The induced bias matrix* $C = AA - nA$ *should be equal (or close) to a zero matrix if comparison matrix A is perfectly (or approximately) consistent. That is*

$$C = AA - nA \begin{cases} = 0 & \text{if } a_{ik}a_{kj} = a_{ij} \\ \approx 0 & \text{if } a_{ik}a_{kj} \approx a_{ij} \end{cases} \tag{3.1}$$

where A is the original PCM while a_{ij} *represents the values of PCM. The "n" denotes the order of PCM.*

Proof. Let A be a $n \times n$ pair-wise matrix (n rows, n columns), and B also be a $n \times n$ matrix. Multiply A to B, then the product C is also a matrix with n rows and n columns, that is,

$$C_{n\times n} = A_{n\times n} B_{n\times n} \tag{3.2}$$

From the theorem of matrix multiplication, we have:

$$c_{ij} = \sum_{k=1}^{n} a_{ik} \cdot b_{kj} \tag{3.3}$$

where c_{ij} represents the element in the ith row and j^{th} column of matrix C.
   Likewise, multiply A to A, the product B becomes:

$$B_{n\times n} = A_{n\times n} A_{n\times n} \tag{3.4}$$

Applying formula (3.2) and (3.3) to formula (3.4), obviously we get

$$b_{ij} = \sum_{k=1}^{n} a_{ik} \cdot a_{kj} \tag{3.5}$$

where b_{ij} denotes the element with i^{th} row and j^{th} column in matrix B.

If the reciprocal pairwise comparison matrix A is perfectly consistent, then there is $a_{ik}a_{kj} = a_{ij}$ for all i, j and k. That is

$$a_{ik}a_{kj} = \frac{w_i}{w_k} \cdot \frac{w_k}{w_j} = \frac{w_i}{w_j} = a_{ij} \qquad (3.6)$$

where w_i, w_j, and w_k denote the weigh vector of attributes a_i, a_j and a_k respectively. Applying formula (3.6) to formula (3.5), then we have:

$$b_{ij} = \sum_{k=1}^{n} a_{ik} \cdot a_{kj} = na_{ij} \qquad (3.7)$$

Therefore all elements of the induced bias matrix C are equal to zero and the induced bias matrix C is a zero matrix.

$$C = AA - nA = (na_{ij})_{n \times n} - n(a_{ij})_{n \times n} = (0)_{n \times n} \qquad (3.8)$$

Likewise, if pairwise comparison matrix (PCM hereinafter) A is approximately consistent, then there is $a_{ik}a_{kj} \approx a_{ij}$ for all i, j and k, the above two equations become:

$$b_{ij} = \sum_{k=1}^{n} a_{ik} \cdot a_{kj} \approx na_{ij} \qquad (3.9)$$

Then the formula (3.8) becomes:

$$C = AA - nA \approx (na_{ij})_{n \times n} - n(a_{ij})_{n \times n} = (0)_{n \times n} \qquad (3.10)$$

Therefore most of the entries in the induced bias matrix C are close to zero and the induced bias matrix C is also close to a zero matrix if PCM is approximately consistent. □

In order to demonstrate how the theorem works in our inconsistency identification method, a 3×3 pairwise matrix (3 rows, 3 columns) is introduced as an example, and the processes of matrix multiplication are exhibited below. Let $A = (a_{ij})$ be a 3×3 pairwise matrix:

$$A = \begin{pmatrix} a_{11} & a_{12} & a_{13} \\ a_{21} & a_{22} & a_{23} \\ a_{31} & a_{32} & a_{33} \end{pmatrix} \qquad (3.11)$$

Then $B = A \cdot A = \begin{pmatrix} a_{11} & a_{12} & a_{13} \\ a_{21} & a_{22} & a_{23} \\ a_{31} & a_{32} & a_{33} \end{pmatrix} \cdot \begin{pmatrix} a_{11} & a_{12} & a_{13} \\ a_{21} & a_{22} & a_{23} \\ a_{31} & a_{32} & a_{33} \end{pmatrix}$

$$= \begin{pmatrix} a_{11} \cdot a_{11} + a_{12} \cdot a_{21} + a_{13} \cdot a_{31} & a_{11} \cdot a_{12} + a_{12} \cdot a_{22} \\ a_{21} \cdot a_{11} + a_{22} \cdot a_{21} + a_{23} \cdot a_{31} & a_{21} \cdot a_{12} + a_{22} \cdot a_{22} \\ a_{31} \cdot a_{11} + a_{32} \cdot a_{21} + a_{33} \cdot a_{31} & a_{31} \cdot a_{12} + a_{32} \cdot a_{22} \end{pmatrix}$$

$$\begin{pmatrix} + a_{13} \cdot a_{32} & a_{11} \cdot a_{13} + a_{12} \cdot a_{23} + a_{13} \cdot a_{33} \\ + a_{23} \cdot a_{32} & a_{21} \cdot a_{13} + a_{22} \cdot a_{23} + a_{23} \cdot a_{33} \\ + a_{33} \cdot a_{32} & a_{31} \cdot a_{13} + a_{32} \cdot a_{23} + a_{33} \cdot a_{33} \end{pmatrix} \tag{3.12}$$

If A is perfectly consistent, then

$$b_{ij} = \sum_{k=1}^{3} a_{ik} \cdot a_{kj} = 3a_{ij} \tag{3.13}$$

So $B = A \cdot A = \begin{pmatrix} 3a_{11} & 3a_{12} & 3a_{13} \\ 3a_{21} & 3a_{22} & 3a_{23} \\ 3a_{31} & 3a_{32} & 3a_{33} \end{pmatrix} = 3A \tag{3.14}$

And $C = A \cdot A - 3A = \begin{pmatrix} 0 & 0 & 0 \\ 0 & 0 & 0 \\ 0 & 0 & 0 \end{pmatrix} \tag{3.15}$

The scale values in pairwise matrix are given by experts according to their judgments and expertise. To be consistent, the rank can be transitive but the values of judgment do not necessarily follow the multiplication formula $a_{ik}a_{kj} = a_{ij}$ (Saaty 1991, 2001b). Obviously, the closer the values of $a_{ik}a_{kj}$ to the value of a_{ij}, the more consistent the comparison matrix is.

Hence, the values of $a_{ik}a_{kj}$ should be as close to the value of a_{ij} as possible. If the consistency index of this matrix is less than 0.1, as the average of express $\sum_{k=1}^{n} a_{ik} \cdot a_{kj}$ is close to the value of a_{ij}, no correction of judgment matrix is needed. The values of all elements are close to zero in the induced bias matrix C.

If the absolute value of element in the induced bias matrix is much larger than zero, it indicates that the deviation between the average of $\sum_{k=1}^{n} a_{ik} \cdot a_{kj}$ and the value of a_{ij} is not negligible. It shows that either some of the values of $a_{ik}a_{kj}$ are too large or the corresponding value of a_{ij} is too small. The deviation could be observed in the induced bias matrix C, and the possible error elements could also be identified by the vectors dot product method. The decision maker may revise his judgments once the deviation elements are identified.

In the *Theorem 3.2,* the correctness of the IBMM for consistency case is proved mathematically. Based on the *Theorem 3.2* and the above analysis, in the following, the critical theorem of IBMM for inconsistency identification is proposed and proved mathematically by maximum eigenvalue method and by contradiction method.

Theorem 3.3. *There must be some inconsistent elements in the induced bias matrix (IBM) C deviating far away from zero if the pairwise matrix is inconsistent. Especially, any row or column of matrix C contains at least one positive element.*

1. Proof by maximum eigenvalue method. We prove that if the PCM A is inconsistent, then the induced bias matrix $C = AA - nA$ cannot be zero. More precisely, we show that any row of C contains at least one nonzero element.

It is known, see e.g. Saaty (1980), that for the maximal eigenvalue $\lambda_{\max}$ of A we have $\lambda_{\max} \geq n$, and the corresponding unique eigenvector $\omega_{\max}$ is a positive vector. Furthermore, A is consistent if and only if $\lambda_{\max} = n$. By applying

$$A\,\omega_{\max} = \lambda_{\max}\omega_{\max} \qquad (3.16)$$

at the appropriate places, we obtain

$$C\omega_{\max} = (AA - nA)\,\omega_{\max} = \lambda_{\max}A\omega_{\max} - n\lambda_{\max}\omega_{\max}$$

$$= \lambda_{\max}^2\omega_{\max} - n\lambda_{\max}\omega_{\max} = \lambda_{\max}\left(\lambda_{\max} - n\right)\omega_{\max} \qquad (3.17)$$

Since $\lambda_{\max} > n$, we get that $C\omega_{\max}$ is a positive vector, consequently, C cannot have any row containing only zeros. Moreover, since both $C\omega_{\max}$ and $\omega_{\max}$ are positive vectors, any row or column of C must contain at least one positive element. □

2. Proof by contradiction. It has been proved previously that if a reciprocal pairwise comparison matrix (RPCM) is perfectly consistent, that is, $a_{ij} = a_{ik}a_{kj}$ for all i, j, k, then we can get

$$c_{ij} = \sum_{k=1}^{n} a_{ik} \cdot a_{kj} - na_{ij} = na_{ij} - na_{ij} = 0 \qquad (3.18)$$

If a PCM A is inconsistent, then $a_{ij} \neq a_{ik}a_{kj}$ at least holds for one of the $i, j, k (i, j, k = 1, 2, \cdots, n)$. Moreover, it can be shown that if A is inconsistent, then for any i there exist j and k such that $a_{ij} \neq a_{ik}a_{kj}$, see *Corollary 2* in Bozóki et al. (2011). Now assume a PCM A is inconsistent, but the i-th row of the induced bias matrix C contains only nonpositive elements. Then $a_{ij} \neq a_{ik}a_{kj}$ with some j and k, and $c_{i1} \leq 0, c_{i2} \leq 0, \ldots, c_{in} \leq 0$. We can get the following inequalities:

$$\begin{cases} c_{i1} = \displaystyle\sum_{k=1}^{n} a_{ik}a_{k1} - na_{i1} \leq 0 \\[2ex] c_{i2} = \displaystyle\sum_{k=1}^{n} a_{ik}a_{k2} - na_{i2} \leq 0 \\[2ex] \vdots \\[2ex] c_{in} = \displaystyle\sum_{k=1}^{n} a_{ik}a_{kn} - na_{in} \leq 0 \end{cases} \qquad (3.19)$$

$$\Rightarrow \begin{cases} \dfrac{1}{a_{i1}} \displaystyle\sum_{k=1}^{n} a_{ik}a_{k1} \leq n \\[2ex] \dfrac{1}{a_{i2}} \displaystyle\sum_{k=1}^{n} a_{ik}a_{k2} \leq n \\[2ex] \vdots \\[2ex] \dfrac{1}{a_{in}} \displaystyle\sum_{k=1}^{n} a_{ik}a_{kn} \leq n \end{cases} \qquad (3.20)$$

Add all the inequalities together in the system of inequalities (3.20), we can get

$$\frac{1}{a_{i1}} \sum_{k=1}^{n} a_{ik}a_{k1} + \frac{1}{a_{i2}} \sum_{k=1}^{n} a_{ik}a_{k2} + \cdots + \frac{1}{a_{in}} \sum_{k=1}^{n} a_{ik}a_{kn} \leq n^2 \qquad (3.21)$$

$$\Rightarrow \sum_{k=1}^{n} \frac{1}{a_{i1}} a_{ik}a_{k1} + \sum_{k=1}^{n} \frac{1}{a_{i2}} a_{ik}a_{k2} + \cdots + \sum_{k=1}^{n} \frac{1}{a_{in}} a_{ik}a_{kn} \leq n^2 \qquad (3.22)$$

$$\Rightarrow \sum_{j=1}^{n}\sum_{k=1}^{n} \frac{1}{a_{ij}} a_{ik}a_{kj} = \sum_{j=1}^{n}\sum_{k=1}^{n} a_{kj} \frac{a_{ik}}{a_{ij}} \leq n^2 \qquad (3.23)$$

To easily observe the rule of each term in the sum, the inequality (3.22) or (3.23) can be unfolded to the following matrix form,

$$\frac{1}{a_{i1}}a_{i1}a_{11} + \frac{1}{a_{i1}}a_{i2}a_{21} + \frac{1}{a_{i1}}a_{i3}a_{31} + \cdots + \frac{1}{a_{i1}}a_{ii}a_{i1} + \cdots + \frac{1}{a_{i1}}a_{ij}a_{j1} + \cdots + \frac{1}{a_{i1}}a_{in}a_{n1} +$$

$$\frac{1}{a_{i2}}a_{i1}a_{12} + \frac{1}{a_{i2}}a_{i2}a_{22} + \frac{1}{a_{i2}}a_{i3}a_{32} + \cdots + \frac{1}{a_{i2}}a_{ii}a_{i2} + \cdots + \frac{1}{a_{i2}}a_{ij}a_{j2} + \cdots + \frac{1}{a_{i2}}a_{in}a_{n2} +$$

$$\frac{1}{a_{i3}}a_{i1}a_{13} + \frac{1}{a_{i3}}a_{i2}a_{23} + \frac{1}{a_{i3}}a_{i3}a_{33} + \cdots + \frac{1}{a_{i3}}a_{ii}a_{i3} + \cdots + \frac{1}{a_{i3}}a_{ij}a_{j3} + \cdots + \frac{1}{a_{i3}}a_{in}a_{n3} +$$

$$\vdots \qquad \vdots \qquad \vdots$$

$$\frac{1}{a_{ii}}a_{i1}a_{1i} + \frac{1}{a_{ii}}a_{i2}a_{2i} + \frac{1}{a_{ii}}a_{i3}a_{3i} + \cdots + \frac{1}{a_{ii}}a_{ii}a_{ii} + \cdots + \frac{1}{a_{ii}}a_{ij}a_{ji} + \cdots + \frac{1}{a_{ii}}a_{in}a_{ni} +$$

$$\vdots \qquad \vdots \qquad \vdots$$

$$\frac{1}{a_{ij}}a_{i1}a_{1j} + \frac{1}{a_{ij}}a_{i2}a_{2j} + \frac{1}{a_{ij}}a_{i3}a_{3j} + \cdots + \frac{1}{a_{ij}}a_{ii}a_{ij} + \cdots + \frac{1}{a_{ij}}a_{ij}a_{jj} + \cdots + \frac{1}{a_{ij}}a_{in}a_{nj} +$$

$$\vdots \qquad \vdots$$

$$\frac{1}{a_{in}}a_{i1}a_{1n} + \frac{1}{a_{in}}a_{i2}a_{2n} + \frac{1}{a_{in}}a_{i3}a_{3n} + \cdots + \frac{1}{a_{in}}a_{ii}a_{in} + \cdots + \frac{1}{a_{in}}a_{ij}a_{jn} + \cdots + \frac{1}{a_{in}}a_{in}a_{nn} \le n^2$$

$$(3.24)$$

Since matrix A is a reciprocal matrix, that is, $a_{kj} = \frac{1}{a_{jk}}$ and $a_{kj} > 0, a_{ij} > 0, a_{ik} > 0$, and it can easily be seen from the expansion inequality (3.24) that any of the above inequalities (3.20), (3.21), (3.22), and (3.23) can be simplified as the following inequality:

$$n + \sum_{k>j}\left(a_{kj}\frac{a_{ik}}{a_{ij}} + a_{jk}\frac{a_{ij}}{a_{ik}}\right) \le n^2 \tag{3.25}$$

$$\Rightarrow \sum_{k>j}\left(a_{kj}\frac{a_{ik}}{a_{ij}} + a_{jk}\frac{a_{ij}}{a_{ik}}\right) \le n^2 - n \tag{3.26}$$

Since there are $\frac{n(n-1)}{2}$ sum term at the left side of the inequality (3.26), and $a_{kj}\frac{a_{ik}}{a_{ij}} + a_{jk}\frac{a_{ij}}{a_{ik}} = a_{kj}\frac{a_{ik}}{a_{ij}} + \frac{1}{a_{kj}\frac{a_{ik}}{a_{ij}}} \ge 2$, the inequality (3.26) holds if and only if $a_{kj}\frac{a_{ik}}{a_{ij}} = 1$, namely, $a_{ij} = a_{ik}a_{kj}$ for all j and k. However, this result contradicts the previous assumption that $a_{ij} \ne a_{ik}a_{kj}$ for some j and k. Therefore, one of the inequalities, at least, does not hold, thus, (3.26) holds with $>$ sign. This entails that at least one of elements in the i-th row of the induced bias matrix C is positive. $\square$

Based on the above two proofs for rows, the same proofs for columns can also be induced. If A is a pairwise comparison matrix with the reciprocal property, the transpose of A is also a pairwise comparison matrix with the reciprocal property. In addition, A is consistent if and only if the transpose of A is consistent.

The transpose of the IBM C generated by A is the IBM generated by the transpose of A. Consequently, if C is inconsistent, any column of C contains at least one positive element. The same statement for the rows was stated earlier.

To demonstrate the principles of *Theorem 3.2* and *Theorem 3.3*, a 3×3 reciprocal pairwise matrix with errors is introduced as an example. Let $A = (a_{ij})$ be a 3×3 pairwise matrix and without loss of generality, let us assume that some errors are introduced as

$$a'_{12} = ea_{12}, \quad a'_{13} = (2 - e)\, a_{12} \tag{3.27}$$

where the e denotes error. Since $a_{ij} > 0$, the e should satisfy the inequality $0 < e < 2$.

According to the reciprocal condition, the comparisons matrix A should be

$$A = \begin{pmatrix} a_{11} & a'_{12} & a'_{13} \\ a'_{21} & a_{22} & a_{23} \\ a'_{31} & a_{32} & a_{33} \end{pmatrix} = \begin{pmatrix} a_{11} & ea_{12} & (2-e)a_{13} \\ 1/ea_{12} & a_{22} & a_{23} \\ 1/(2-e)a_{13} & a_{32} & a_{33} \end{pmatrix} \tag{3.28}$$

$$\Rightarrow$$

$$AA = \begin{pmatrix} a_{11} & ea_{12} & (2-e)a_{13} \\ 1/ea_{12} & a_{22} & a_{23} \\ 1/(2-e)a_{13} & a_{32} & a_{33} \end{pmatrix} \begin{pmatrix} a_{11} & ea_{12} & (2-e)a_{13} \\ 1/ea_{12} & a_{22} & a_{23} \\ 1/(2-e)a_{13} & a_{32} & a_{33} \end{pmatrix}$$

$$= \begin{pmatrix} a_{11} + 2 & (2+e)a_{12} & (4-e)a_{13} \\ a_{21}/e + a_{21}/e + a_{21}/(2-e) & a_{22} + 2 & (2-e)a_{23}/e + 2a_{23} \\ a_{31}/(2-e) + a_{31}/e + a_{31}/(2-e) & ea_{32}/(2-e) + 2a_{32} & a_{33} + 2 \end{pmatrix}$$

$$= \begin{pmatrix} 3 & (2+e)a_{12} & (4-e)a_{13} \\ (2/e + 1/(2-e))a_{21} & 3 & ((2-e)/e + 2)a_{23} \\ (2/(2-e) + 1/e)a_{31} & (e/(2-e) + 2)a_{32} & 3 \end{pmatrix} \tag{3.29}$$

Note: $\quad a_{21} = \frac{1}{a_{12}}, \quad a_{31} = \frac{1}{a_{13}}, \quad a_{11} = a_{22} = a_{33} = 1$

Apply the proposed method to the induced bias matrix C:

$$C = AA - 3A$$

$$= \begin{pmatrix} 3 & (2+e)a_{12} & (4-e)a_{13} \\ (2/e + 1/(2-e))a_{21} & 3 & ((2-e)/e + 2)a_{23} \\ (2/(2-e) + 1/e)a_{31} & (e/(2-e) + 2)a_{32} & 3 \end{pmatrix}$$

$$-3 \times \begin{pmatrix} a_{11} & ea_{12} & (2-e)a_{13} \\ a_{21}/e & a_{22} & a_{23} \\ a_{31}/(2-e) & a_{32} & a_{33} \end{pmatrix}$$

$$= \begin{pmatrix} 0 & 2(1-e)a_{12} & 2(e-1)a_{13} \\ \frac{2(e-1)}{(2-e)e}a_{21} & 0 & \frac{2(1-e)}{e}a_{23} \\ \frac{2(1-e)}{e(2-e)}a_{31} & \frac{2(e-1)}{2-e}a_{32} & 0 \end{pmatrix}$$

$$(3.30)$$

The result shows that the IBM C is not a zero matrix if there are some errors ($e \neq 1$) in the comparison matrix A.

In order to exhibit the *Theorem 3.2* and *Theorem 3.3* using concrete errors, we can analyze two cases:

1. **Case 1-** comparison matrix A does not have any errors;
2. **Case 2-** comparison matrix A has errors.

Assume $e = 1$ and $e = \frac{1}{2}$ respectively, which means that there is no errors in the comparison matrix A and there is some errors in the comparison matrix A respectively. Then the IBM C is calculated by applying the corresponding error to the formula (3.30). The detailed are showed as follows:

1. **Case 1:** If $e = 1$, then

$$C = A \cdot A - 3A = \begin{pmatrix} 0 & 0 & 0 \\ 0 & 0 & 0 \\ 0 & 0 & 0 \end{pmatrix} \qquad (3.31)$$

According to the *Theorem 3.1*, the pairwise comparison matrix A is perfectly consistent. The result is in accordance with the above assumption.

2. **Case 2:** If $e = \frac{1}{2}$, then the IBM C becomes

$$C = AA - 3A = \begin{pmatrix} 0 & a_{12} & -a_{13} \\ -4a_{21}/3 & 0 & 2a_{23} \\ 4a_{31}/3 & -2/3a_{32} & 0 \end{pmatrix} \qquad (3.32)$$

Obviously, the IBM C is not a zero matrix, which is consistent with the *Theorem 3.3*. From the above results we find that all entries in the main diagonal of the IBM C are equal to zero. This result indicates that the comparison matrix A satisfies the reciprocal condition although it is inconsistent. Therefore, the following theorem can be derived.

Theorem 3.4. *All entries in the main diagonal of the induced bias matrix (IBM) $C = AA - nA$ should be zeroes whether matrix A is consistent or not as long as the comparison matrix A satisfies the reciprocal condition.*

Proofs. According to the principle of matrix multiplication, all values in the main diagonal of the induced bias matrix C can be calculated by the formula (3.33):

$$c_{ii} = \sum_{k=1}^{n} a_{ik} \cdot a_{ki} - na_{ii} \tag{3.33}$$

If $a_{ki} = \frac{1}{a_{ik}}$, *and* $a_{ii} = 1$, then

$$c_{ii} = \sum_{k=1}^{n} a_{ik} \cdot a_{ki} - na_{ii} = \sum_{k=1}^{n} a_{ik} \cdot \frac{1}{a_{ik}} - na_{ii} = n - n = 0, \quad i = 1, 2, \cdots, n$$
$$\tag{3.34}$$

□

The case that the comparison matrix A satisfies the reciprocal condition has been proved previously in the section, the following example will show the case that the comparison matrix A does not satisfy the reciprocal condition.

Once again, we use the 3×3 pairwise matrix $A = (a_{ij})$ with errors as the example and the assumption given in formula (3.28) to prove the second case. Without loss of generality, let us assume a_{21} and a_{31} do not have any errors, then the comparison matrix $A = (a_{ij})$ becomes

$$A = \begin{pmatrix} a_{11} & ea_{12} & (2-e)a_{13} \\ a_{21} & a_{22} & a_{23} \\ a_{31} & a_{32} & a_{33} \end{pmatrix} \tag{3.35}$$

According to the proposed method, the induced bias matrix C becomes:

$$C = \begin{pmatrix} 0 & (2-2e)a_{12} & (2e-2)a_{13} \\ 0 & (e-1)a_{22} & (1-e) \cdot a_{23} \\ 0 & (e-1)a_{32} & (1-e)a_{33} \end{pmatrix} \tag{3.36}$$

Obviously, the elements in the main diagonal of the induced bias matrix C are not equal to zeroes except the situation when there has no errors ($e = 1$). It proofs the comparison matrix A is not reciprocal, which is consistent with the previous assumption.   □

According to *Theorem 3.4*, if matrix A is reciprocal, the diagonal elements of C are 0. However, for the matrix A with order higher than 3, we cannot derive that matrix A must be reciprocal even if the diagonal elements of C are 0. But if the diagonal elements of C are not 0 or contains some nonzero elements, then we can derive that the matrix A does not satisfy the reciprocal condition, and some of the elements at least are not reciprocal. Although the reciprocal property can be checked directly in the matrix A in a simple and exact way, and it seems that there is no need to make it more complicated, it is still an effective way for ANP to exclude the case that the inconsistency is only caused by violating the reciprocal property due to there are plenty of comparison matrices in ANP than in AHP. Moreover, all the values of comparison matrices are normally input manually, and it is sometimes easy to make mistakes and cause the comparison matrices to be inconsistency.

3.2   IBMM for Inconsistent Data Identification and Adjustment

3.2.1   The Basics of the Inconsistency Identification and Adjustment Method

We have previously proved that any row of the IBM C contains at least one non-zero element if the PCM A is inconsistent, that is, $a_{ij} \neq a_{ik}a_{kj}$ holds at least for one group of i, j, k, which means that there is at least one pair of inconsistent elements existing in the original PCM A. Suppose c_{ij}, the element with largest absolute value in the IBM C, is identified. The second step is to analyze that which element makes c_{ij} to be far away from zero. According to the rule of matrix multiplication, the value of c_{ij} is calculated by all values on the ith row and j^{th} column of matrix A and a_{ij}, that is,

$$c_{ij} = \sum_{k=1}^{n} a_{ik} \cdot a_{kj} - na_{ij}$$
$$= a_{i1}a_{1j} - a_{ij} + a_{i2}a_{2j} - a_{ij} + \cdots + a_{ik}a_{kj} - a_{ij} + \cdots + a_{in}a_{nj} - a_{ij} \tag{3.37}$$

Clearly, the farthest value of c_{ij} can be impacted by any term of $a_{ik}a_{kj} - a_{ij}$ on the right side of the sum equality (3.37). In order to identify the inconsistent elements that caused the value of c_{ij} to be far away from zero, the scalar product of vectors in n dimension technique is introduced. The impact of each term can easily be observed by the scalar product of vectors in n dimension technique, that is,

$$b = r_i \cdot c_j^T = (a_{i1}, a_{i2}, \cdots, a_{in}) \cdot (a_{1j}, a_{2j}, \cdots, a_{nj}) = (a_{i1}a_{1j}, a_{i2}a_{2j}, \cdots, a_{in}a_{nj}) \tag{3.38}$$

and

$$f = b - a_{ij} = (a_{i1}a_{1j} - a_{ij}, a_{i2}a_{2j} - a_{ij}, \cdots a_{ik}a_{kj} - a_{ij}, \cdots, a_{in}a_{nj} - a_{ij}) \tag{3.39}$$

If $a_{ij} \neq a_{ik}a_{kj}$, then $a_{ik}a_{kj} - a_{ij} \neq 0$. Therefore, the non-zero element(s), which caused the value of c_{ij} to be far away from zero, can be identified through observing all elements in the bias identifying vector f. In addition, the inequality $a_{ij} \neq a_{ik}a_{kj}$ can be caused by a_{ij} or any $a_{ik}a_{kj}$ $(k = 1, 2, \cdots, n)$ or both.

Obviously, if the inconsistent element is a_{ij}, other elements are consistent. Assume $a_{ik}a_{kj} = a'_{ij} > a_{ij}$, namely, a_{ij} is too small. We can get all values in the bias identifying vector f are positive except $k = i, j$, as $a_{ii}a_{ij} - a_{ij} = 0$ and $a_{ij}a_{jj} - a_{ij} = 0$. Vices versus, if a_{ij} is too large, all the values in the bias identifying vector f will be negative except two values $k = i, j$. Therefore, the "*Method for identifying a_{ij}*" inconsistency identification method was proposed (Ergu et al. 2011a).

Besides, the farthest value of c_{ij} must be caused by some outliers either too large or too small located at the bias identifying vector f, therefore, "*Method for Maximum*" and "*Method for Minimum*" inconsistency identification methods were proposed (Ergu et al. 2011b).

In order to further identify the inconsistent element for those elements whose values are close to the largest or smallest simultaneously, therefore, the "*Method of matrix order reduction*" inconsistency identification method was proposed (Ergu et al. 2011b).

3.2.2 The Processes of Inconsistency Identification and Adjustment Method

Assuming the pairwise comparison matrix A with n rows and n columns is inconsistent. Based on the above analysis of the basics of inconsistency identification and adjustment method, the processes to identify inconsistent elements of comparison matrix as well as the methods to analyze and adjust those elements are proposed as the following three major steps which include 7 specific identifying steps.

Step I: Identify the location of inconsistent element whose absolute value is the largest in the induced pairwise comparison matrix.

Step 1: Construct an induced matrix C with the following formula:

$$C = AA - nA$$

Step 2: Identify the largest absolute value(s) of elements deviating farthest from zero in the induced matrix C, and record the location. For instance, suppose c_{ij} is such an element in matrix C and the location is i^{th} row and j^{th} column.

Step II: Identify the potential inconsistent elements by the bias identifying vector.

Step 3: Let the ith row of the original pairwise comparison matrix A be represented as a row vector $r_i = (a_{i1}, a_{i2}, \cdots, a_{in})$ and the jth column of the same matrix as a column vector $c_j^T = (a_{1j}, a_{2j}, \cdots, a_{nj})^T$, where c_j^T is the transpose vector of column vector c_j.

Step 4:   Calculate the scalar product of the vectors r_i and c_i^T in n dimension. The dot product b of the two vectors becomes:

$$b = r_i \cdot c_j^T = (a_{i1}, a_{i2}, \cdots, a_{in}) \cdot (a_{1j}, a_{2j}, \cdots, a_{nj}) = (a_{i1}a_{1j}, a_{i2}a_{2j}, \cdots, a_{in}a_{nj})$$

Step 5:   Compute the deviation elements which are far away from a_{ij} in vector b by the following formula. Let f be the bias identifying vector henceforth.

$$f = b - a_{ij} = (a_{i1}a_{1j} - a_{ij}, a_{i2}a_{2j} - a_{ij}, \cdots a_{ik}a_{kj} - a_{ij}, \cdots, a_{in}a_{nj} - a_{ij})$$

Step III: Identify the inconsistent elements using the identification method and the method of matrix order reduction.

Step 6:   Identify the error elements in pairwise matrix A that might cause the inconsistency by bias identifying vector f using the following three principal identification methods and the method of matrix order reduction.

(a) *Method of Maximum:* If more absolute values in vector f are around zero, and fewer values are deviating from zero, then identify the largest value in vector f. If there are other values close to the largest one, then identify those elements simultaneously.

(b) *Method of Minimum:* If more absolute values of elements in vector f are far away from zero, and fewer values are close to zero, or equal to zero, then identify the smallest value in vector f. If there are other values close or equal to the smallest one, then identify those elements simultaneously.

(c) *Method for identifying a_{ij}:*

1. If the largest value in induced matrix C is negative, then a_{ij} is too large.
2. If there are only two zeroes where the location is i^{th} and j^{th} in bias vector f, and others are positive, then a_{ij} is too small. Otherwise, a_{ij} is too large. In the former case, if a_{ij} is already close to the maximum scale 9, then identify the next largest value in the induced matrix C, and further identify other inconsistent elements using method of matrix order reduction.

Assume the bias value of $a_{ik}a_{kj} - a_{ij}$ in bias vector f is the largest positive one, and others are around zero. Clearly, $a_{ik}a_{kj}$ is larger than a_{ij}, and others are equal or close to a_{ij}. Then, there are following four conditions.

Condition 1: a_{ik} is too large;
Condition 2: a_{kj} is too large;
Condition 3: Both a_{ik} and a_{kj} are too large; or
Condition 4: a_{ij} is too small.

Given the above conditions, the element to be adjusted could be identified as Step 7:

Step 7: Find the values of c_{ik} and c_{kj} in the induced matrix C according to the following procedures:

Based on our assumption, that is, assume the bias value of $a_{ik}a_{kj} - a_{ij}$ in bias vector f is the largest positive one, then one or both a_{ik} and a_{kj} are too large, therefore it is impossible that $c_{ik} > 0$ and $c_{kj} > 0$ simultaneously.

If $c_{ik} < 0$ and $c_{kj} > 0$, then a_{ik} is too large due to $c_{ik} = \frac{1}{n} \sum_{l=1}^{n} a_{il}a_{lk} - a_{ik}$, and a_{kj} is too small. If a_{ik} is too large, then the decision makers should decrease the value of element a_{ik}, so the value of $a_{ik}a_{kj}$ is closer to the value of a_{ij}.

If $c_{ik} > 0$ and $c_{kj} < 0$, similarly, the decision makers should decrease the value of element a_{kj}, so the value of $a_{ik}a_{kj}$ is closer to the value of a_{ij}.

If $c_{ik} < 0$ and $c_{kj} < 0$, and the bias between both absolute values are too large, then the maximum absolute element can be identified using the inconsistency identification method again.

If $c_{ik} < 0$ and $c_{kj} < 0$, and the bias between both absolute values are close to each other, then the following method of matrix order reduction for pair-wise matrix could be used to identify the bias elements. This method could identify the bias elements accurately and keep the comparison information provided by the experts as much as possible, especially for the pair-wise matrix with high order. The method of matrix order reduction could also identify the elements which are close to the largest or smallest simultaneously.

3.2.2.1 Method of Matrix Order Reduction

As illustrated above, both a_{ik} and a_{kj} are either too large or the value of a_{ij} is too small. It indicates that some attributes or criteria, namely, A_i, A_k or A_j have impacts on other attributes and is an inconsistent element. Therefore, we can test whether it can pass the consistency test or not by removing some attributes one by one from the original pair-wise matrix, which is called method of matrix order reduction. The inconsistent attributes could be identified by this method with the following sub-steps:

Sub-step 1: Test the consistency of the order reduced comparison matrix $A_{(n-1)\times(n-1)}$ by removing the attribute A_k, namely, deleting k^{th} row and k^{th} column from the original pair-wise matrix A.

If the consistency test passed, the attribute A_k is inconsistent while a_{ij} is consistent, then go to sub-step 2 to identify a_{ik} and a_{kj}.

If the consistency test failed, there must be other inconsistent attributes in the order reduced pair-wise matrix. Hence, a_{ij} is inconsistent and the value of a_{ij}

Table 3.1 The identification process for method of matrix order reduction (Sub-step 1–3)

Remove	Test	Might problem	Good	Problem
A_k	✓	a_{ik}, a_{kj}	a_{ij}	
	×	a_{ik}, a_{kj}		a_{ij}
A_i	✓	a_{ik}	a_{kj}	
	×			a_{kj}
A_j	✓	a_{kj}	a_{ik}	
	×			a_{ik}

can be increased so it is closer to the average of $\sum_{k=1}^{n} a_{ik} \cdot a_{kj}$. Meanwhile, both a_{ik} and a_{kj} also might be problematic, and continue to Sub-step2.

Sub-step 2: Test the consistency of the order reduced pair-wise matrix $A_{(n-1) \times (n-1)}$ by removing the attribute A_i from the original pair-wise matrix A.

If the consistency test passed, both attributes A_k and A_j are consistent. There is no need to change a_{kj}. Hence, decrease a_{ik} as a_{ij} was identified in Sub-step 1.

If the consistency test failed, at least one of the attributes A_k or A_j is inconsistent, then decrease a_{kj}. Meanwhile, a_{ik} might also be inconsistent, and go to Sub-step 3.

Sub-step 3: Test the consistency of order reduced pair-wise matrix $A_{(n-1) \times (n-1)}$ by removing the attribute A_j from the original pair-wise matrix A.

If the consistency test passed, then a_{ik} is consistent; otherwise a_{ik} should be decreased.

If the consistency test failed in both sub-step 2 and sub-step 3, we have to let the decision makers to change both elements a_{ik} and a_{kj} simultaneously.

If the decision makers want to further check whether there exists other inconsistent attributes, we have to test the consistency of the order reduced pair-wise matrix by removing attributes A_i, A_k or A_j simultaneously.

To explain the identification process, Table 3.1 shows the identification process of a_{ik}, a_{kj} and a_{ij}. In Table 3.1, "Remove" represents removing the corresponding attributes. "Test" denotes the consistency test for the order reduced pair-wise matrix. "Might Problem" stands for the elements might have inconsistent problem. "Good" denotes the elements are consistent. "Problem" denotes the elements are inconsistent. "×" denotes the consistency test failed while "✓" stands for a passed consistency test. A_i, A_k and A_j stand for three different attributes.

3.2.3   Fast Inconsistency Identification and Adjustment Method

Some general inconsistency identification methods have been presented previously. In Ergu et al. (2011f), one fast inconsistency identification and adjustment method was proposed for some special cases that there exists only one pair of inconsistent elements in the original PCM.

Assume that PCM A is inconsistent, and there is one pair of inconsistent elements a_{ip} and its corresponding reciprocal element $a_{pi} = \frac{1}{a_{ip}}$, while other elements are consistent, namely, $a_{ik}a_{kj} = a_{ij}$ for all k except $k = p$ ($a_{ip}a_{pj} \neq a_{ij}$). Therefore, the two inconsistent elements are elements at the ith and p^{th} rows, and the pth and i^{th} column. According to the rule of matrix multiplication, all elements, which are located at the ith, p^{th} rows, and the ith, p^{th} column in the induced bias matrix $C = AA - nA$, will be impacted by a_{ip} and a_{pi}. Since it is assumed that $a_{ik}a_{kj} = a_{ij}$ ($k \neq p; j \neq p,$) and $a_{ik}a_{kp} \neq a_{ip}$, suppose $a_{ik}a_{kp} = a'_{ip}$, all the values in the ith row of the IBM C can be computed by formula (3.37), that is,

For the ith row:

$$c_{ij} = \sum_{k=1}^{n} a_{ik} \cdot a_{kj} - na_{ij} = \sum_{k=1,\neq p}^{n} a_{ik} \cdot a_{kj} + a_{ip}a_{pj} - na_{ij}, \quad j = 1, 2, \cdots, n$$

$$= \begin{cases} (n-1)a_{ij} + a_{ip}a_{pj} - na_{ij} = a_{ip}a_{pj} - a_{ij}; & j \neq i, p \\ (n-1) + 1 - n = 0; & j = i \\ (n-2)a'_{ip} + a_{ii}a_{ip} + a_{ip}a_{pp} - na_{ip} = (n-2)\left(a'_{ip} - a_{ip}\right); & j = p \end{cases}$$

$$(3.40)$$

In order to analyze the sign change of each element on the ith row, the equalities in (3.40) are further unfolded, as shown below.

$$\begin{cases} c_{i1} = a_{ip}a_{p1} - a_{i1} \\ c_{i2} = a_{ip}a_{p2} - a_{i2} \\ \quad \vdots \\ c_{ii} = 0 \\ \quad \vdots \\ c_{ip} = (n-1)a'_{ip} + a_{ii}a_{ip} + a_{ip}a_{pp} - na_{ip} = (n-2)(a'_{ip} - a_{ip}) \\ \quad \vdots \\ c_{in} = a_{ip}a_{pn} - a_{in} \end{cases} \qquad (3.41)$$

If $a_{ip} \uparrow$: then

$$
\begin{cases}
c_{i1} = a_{ip}a_{p1} - a_{i1} > 0 \\[2mm]
c_{i2} = a_{ip}a_{p2} - a_{i2} > 0 \\[2mm]
\quad\vdots \\[2mm]
c_{ii} = 0 \\[2mm]
\quad\vdots \\[2mm]
c_{ip} = (n-1)\,a'_{ip} + a_{ii}a_{ip} + a_{ip}a_{pp} - na_{ip} = (n-2)\,(a'_{ip} - a_{ip}) < 0 \\[2mm]
\quad\vdots \\[2mm]
c_{in} = a_{ip}a_{pn} - a_{in} > 0
\end{cases}
\tag{3.42}
$$

If $a_{ip} \downarrow$: then

$$
\begin{cases}
c_{i1} = a_{ip}a_{p1} - a_{i1} < 0 \\[2mm]
c_{i2} = a_{ip}a_{p2} - a_{i2} < 0 \\[2mm]
\quad\vdots \\[2mm]
c_{ii} = 0 \\[2mm]
\quad\vdots \\[2mm]
c_{ip} = (n-1)\,a'_{ip} + a_{ii}a_{ip} + a_{ip}a_{pp} - na_{ip} = (n-2)\,(a'_{ip} - a_{ip}) > 0 \\[2mm]
\quad\vdots \\[2mm]
c_{in} = a_{ip}a_{pn} - a_{in} < 0
\end{cases}
\tag{3.43}
$$

where the symbols "$\uparrow$" and "$\downarrow$" denote "increase" and "decrease" respectively (hereinafter).

Likewise, for the pth row:

$$
c_{pj} = \sum_{k=1}^{n} a_{pk} \cdot a_{kj} - na_{pj} = \sum_{k=1,\neq i}^{n} a_{pk} \cdot a_{kj} + a_{pi}a_{ij} - na_{pj}, \quad j = 1, 2, \cdots, n
$$

$$
= \begin{cases}
(n-1)\,a_{pj} + a_{pi}a_{ij} - na_{pj} = a_{pi}a_{ij} - a_{pj}; & j \neq i, p \\[2mm]
0; & j = p \\[2mm]
(n-1)\,a'_{pj} + a_{pi}a_{ii} + a_{pp}a_{pi} - na_{pi} = (n-2)\,(a'_{pi} - a_{pi}); & j = i
\end{cases}
\tag{3.44}
$$

Therefore, if $a_{ip} \uparrow$, then $a_{pi} = \frac{1}{a_{ip}} \downarrow$,

$$
c_{pj} = \begin{cases} (n-1)\,a_{pj} + a_{pi}a_{ij} - na_{pj} = a_{pi}a_{ij} - a_{pj} < 0; & j \neq i, p \\ 0; & j = p \\ (n-1)\,a'_{pj} + a_{pi}a_{ii} + a_{pp}a_{pi} - na_{pi} = (n-2)\left(a'_{pi} - a_{pi}\right) > 0; & j = i \end{cases}
$$
(3.45)

Likewise, if $a_{ip} \downarrow$, then $a_{pi} = \frac{1}{a_{ip}} \uparrow$,

$$
c_{pj} = \begin{cases} (n-1)\,a_{pj} + a_{pi}a_{ij} - na_{pj} = a_{pi}a_{ij} - a_{pj} > 0; & j \neq i, p \\ 0; & j = p \\ (n-1)\,a'_{pj} + a_{pi}a_{ii} + a_{pp}a_{pi} - na_{pi} = (n-2)\left(a'_{pi} - a_{pi}\right) < 0; & j = i \end{cases}
$$
(3.46)

If $a_{ip} \uparrow$, all values on the ith row of IBM C will be more than zeroes ($c_{ij} > 0, j = 1, 2, \cdots, n$ *and* $j \neq p$) except $c_{ip} < 0$, and all values on the pth row of IBM C will be less than zeroes ($c_{ij} < 0, j = 1, 2, \cdots, n$ *and* $j \neq p$) except $c_{ip} > 0$. Therefore, only the elements on the ith row and p^{th} row are non-zeroes, and the sign form of the values on the ith row and p^{th} row of the IBM C can be derived, as shown in the following matrix,

$$
\begin{pmatrix} & \overset{i^{th}}{} & \overset{p^{th}}{} & & \\ + \cdots + 0 & + \cdots - & + \cdots + & i^{th} \\ - \cdots - + & - \cdots 0 & - \cdots - & p^{th} \end{pmatrix}
$$
(3.47)

Likewise, the signs of each element on the ith column and p^{th} column can be derived similarly. That is,

$$c_{ji} = \sum_{k=1}^{n} a_{jk} \cdot a_{ki} - na_{ji} = \sum_{k=1,\neq p}^{n} a_{jk} \cdot a_{ki} + a_{jp}a_{pi} - na_{ji}, \quad j = 1, 2, \cdots, n$$

$$= \begin{cases} (n-1)\,a_{ji} + a_{jp}a_{pi} - na_{ji} = a_{jp}a_{pi} - a_{ji}; & j \neq p, i \\ 0; & j = i \\ (n-1)\,a'_{pi} + a_{pi}a_{ii} + a_{pp}a_{pi} - na_{pi} = (n-2)\left(a'_{pi} - a_{pi}\right); & j = p \end{cases}$$
$$(3.48)$$

if $a_{ip} \uparrow, a_{pi} = \frac{1}{a_{ip}} \downarrow,$

$$c_{ji} = \begin{cases} (n-1)\,a_{ji} + a_{jp}a_{pi} - na_{ji} = a_{jp}a_{pi} - a_{ji} < 0; & j \neq p, i \\ 0; & j = i \\ (n-1)\,a'_{pi} + a_{pi}a_{ii} + a_{pp}a_{pi} - na_{pi} = (n-2)\left(a'_{pi} - a_{pi}\right) > 0; & j = p \end{cases}$$
$$(3.49)$$

For the pth column,

$$c_{jp} = \sum_{k=1}^{n} a_{jk} \cdot a_{kp} - na_{jp} = \sum_{k=1,\neq i}^{n} a_{jk} \cdot a_{kp} + a_{ji}a_{ip} - na_{jp}, \quad j = 1, 2, \cdots, n$$

$$= \begin{cases} (n-1)\,a_{jp} + a_{ji}a_{ip} - na_{jp} = a_{ji}a_{ip} - a_{jp}; & j \neq p, i \\ 0; & j = p \\ (n-1)\,a'_{ip} + a_{ii}a_{ip} + a_{ip}a_{pp} - na_{ip} = (n-2)\left(a'_{ip} - a_{ip}\right); & j = i \end{cases}$$
$$(3.50)$$

if $a_{ip} \uparrow,$

$$c_{jp} = \begin{cases} (n-1)\,a_{jp} + a_{ji}a_{ip} - na_{jp} = a_{ji}a_{ip} - a_{jp} > 0; & j \neq p, i \\ 0; & j = p \\ (n-1)\,a'_{ip} + a_{ii}a_{ip} + a_{ip}a_{pp} - na_{ip} = (n-2)\left(a'_{ip} - a_{ip}\right) < 0; & j = i \end{cases}$$
$$(3.51)$$

Therefore, the sign forms of the elements on the ith and p^{th} columns of the IBM C can be obtained, as shown in (3.52)

$$
\begin{pmatrix}
\overset{i^{th}}{-} & \overset{p^{th}}{+} \\
\vdots & \vdots \\
- \cdots + \\
0 & - \\
- & + \\
+ \cdots & 0 \\
- & + \\
\vdots & \vdots \\
- & +
\end{pmatrix}
\begin{matrix} \\ \\ \\ i^{th} \\ \\ p^{th} \\ \\ \\ \end{matrix}
\tag{3.52}
$$

To sum up, if a_{ip} ↑, the signs of all the values, which are located at the ith row and the ith column, the pth row and p^{th} column, become:

$$
\begin{pmatrix}
\overset{i^{th}}{-} & \overset{p^{th}}{+} \\
\vdots & \vdots \\
- & + \\
+ \cdots + \; 0 \; + & - \; + \cdots + \\
- & + \\
- \cdots - \; + \; - & 0 \; - \cdots - \\
- & + \\
\vdots & \vdots \\
- & +
\end{pmatrix}
\begin{matrix} \\ \\ \\ i^{th} \\ \\ p^{th} \\ \\ \\ \end{matrix}
\tag{3.53}
$$

Therefore, we can obtain the following fast inconsistency identification method:

3.2.3.1   Method of Non-Zero Rows (Columns) and Signs Identification

If there are two rows (the ith row and the pth row) and two columns (the ith column and p^{th} column) with non-zeroes, and other elements are zero, the inconsistent elements must be a_{ip} and a_{pi}.

If $c_{ip} < 0$ and other elements located at the ith row or p^{th} column are more than zeroes, a_{ip} is too large and should be decreased. Vice versus, a_{ip} is too small and should be increased.

If $c_{pi} > 0$ and other elements located at the pth row or i^{th} column are less than zeroes, a_{ip} is too large and should be decreased. Vice versus, a_{ip} is too small and should be increased.

In addition,

$$c_{ip} = \sum_{k=1}^{n} a_{ik} \cdot a_{kp} - na_{ip} = \sum_{k=1,\neq i,p}^{n} a_{ik} \cdot a_{kp} + a_{ii}a_{ip} + a_{pp}a_{ip} - na_{ip} \quad (3.54)$$

To make the PCM A be consistent, the value of c_{ip} should be equal to zero. Therefore, inconsistent element a_{ip} can be adjusted by formula (3.55).

$$a_{ip} = \frac{1}{n-2} \sum_{k=1,\neq i,p}^{n} a_{ik} \cdot a_{kp} \quad (3.55)$$

In this case, since there is only one pair of inconsistent elements, a_{ip} and a_{pi} in the PCM, any $a_{ik}a_{kp} = a'_{ip}(k \neq i, p,)$ can be used as the revised value of a_{ip}.

3.3 Illustrative Examples

3.3.1 Illustrative Examples for General Inconsistency Identification and Adjustment Method

In order to test and compare the inconsistency identification method illustrated above with others methods, Ergu et al. (2011b) applied the proposed IBMM to some public-domain examples. The first example is a pairwise matrix with unacceptable CI, which was introduced in Liu (1999). The second example that covers different types of errors in pairwise comparison matrices is provided by an anonymous reviewer of Ergu et al. (2011b). The third example was used by Iida (2009) as an example of ordinality consistency test, which was first introduced in (Kwiesielewicz and Uden 2002) as an example of a pair-wise comparison matrix with C.R is 0.1055. In addition, a new pairwise matrix was generated by adding an attribute with random value in the third example to test the proposed inconsistency identification method. Finally, an example, which was introduced by Cao et al. (2008) to compare their heuristic inconsistency modifying approach with Xu and Wei (1999)'s, is also introduced to demonstrate that the proposed IBMM can not only preserve more original comparison information than others but also identify the inconsistent elements easier and quicker. Besides, with this example we also want to demonstrate the identification process for some special situations in the original comparison matrix mentioned in Method for adjusting a_{ij} section.

Example 3.1. The 4×4 pair-wise comparison matrix A is inconsistent with C.R $= 0.173 > 0.1$.

$$A = \begin{pmatrix} 1 & 1/9 & 3 & 1/5 \\ 9 & 1 & 5 & 2 \\ 1/3 & 1/5 & 1 & 1/2 \\ 5 & 1/2 & 2 & 1 \end{pmatrix}$$

The proposed IBMM is applied to test this pair-wise comparison matrix following (Step 1)–(Step 7) in Section 3.2.2 using MATLAB.

Step 1. The induced matrix $C = A * A - 4 * A$ is

$$\begin{pmatrix} 0 & 0.4778 & -5.0444 & 1.3222 \\ -6.3333 & 0 & 21.0000 & 0.3000 \\ 3.6333 & -0.1130 & 0 & -0.5333 \\ -4.8333 & -0.0444 & 13.5000 & 0 \end{pmatrix}$$

Step 2. The largest value in matrix C is 21, where location is second row and third column.

Step 3. Draw out all the values in second row and third column of pair-wise matrix A, that is

$$r_2 = (9\ 1\ 5\ 2), \text{ and } c_3^T = (3\ 5\ 1\ 2)$$

Step 4. The scalar product b of the vectors r_2 and c_3^T in the dimension 4, that is

$$b = r_2 \cdot c_3^T = (27\ 5\ 5\ 4)$$

Step 5. The bias identifying vector f is

$$f = b - a_{23} = (22\ 0\ 0\ -1)$$

Step 6. The value, 22, is the largest one far from zero, and others are zero or close to zero. It indicates that $a_{23} = 5$ is probably correct while $22 = a_{21}a_{13} - a_{23}$ is the inconsistent element. Therefore, we identified $a_{21}a_{13}$ may have problem.

Step 7. As $c_{21} = -6.3333 < 0$ and $c_{13} = -5.0444 < 0$, whose values are close to each other, the corresponding elements a_{21} and a_{13} are too large. Then, the method of matrix order reduction is applied to identify a_{21} and a_{13}.

Sub-step 1. Remove second row and second column from pair-wise matrix A, and do the consistency test, the $\lambda_{max} = 3.4683$, and $C.R. = 0.3 > 0.1$, the test failed. Check a_{13}, and decrease the value of a_{13} and let the product value of $a_{21}a_{13}$ as close to $a_{23} = 5$ as possible.

Sub-step 2. Remove third row and third column from the pair-wise matrix A, and do the consistency test, the $\lambda_{max} = 3.0012$, and $C.R. = 0 < 0.1$, the test passed. So no further correction is needed for a_{21}.

Sub-step 3. Remove first row and first column from pair-wise matrix A, and do the consistency test, the $\lambda_{\max} = 3.0055$, and $C.R. = 0 < 0.1$, the test passed. No correction is needed for a_{23}. Besides, according to the result in Step 5, a_{23} is consistent.

Most of the time, we don't need to finish all Sub-steps for inconsistency test, except some situations when complicated inconsistency identification and adjustment is needed.

As $a_{23} = 5$ and $a_{21} = 9$ are given in the original pair-wise matrix, let $a_{13} = 1/2$, and $a_{31} = 2$, then $a_{21}a_{13}$ is equal to 4.5, which is very close to $a_{23} = 5$. Replace the two values from comparison matrix, and the consistency test passed with $C.R. = 0.0028 < 0.1$. This result is the same as the one in (Liu 1999). However, in Liu's method (Liu 1999), two matrices are needed to identify the inconsistent elements including an induced matrix based on priority vector derived from the comparison matrix and another deviation matrix. In the proposed method, there is no need to construct a new induced matrix based on the priority vector derived from the pairwise matrix and another deviation matrix to identify the inconsistent elements.

Example 3.2. To demonstrate such case that the example covers different types of errors in pair-wise comparison matrices, that is, there is more than one largest value which is equal to each other in the induced bias matrix C, the following inconsistent comparison matrix with an outlying judgment and CR = 1.0242 is introduced.

$$
A = \begin{bmatrix}
1 & 2 & 4 & \frac{1}{8} \\
\frac{1}{2} & 1 & 2 & 4 \\
\frac{1}{4} & \frac{1}{2} & 1 & 2 \\
8 & \frac{1}{4} & \frac{1}{2} & 1
\end{bmatrix}
$$

Step 1. The induced matrix $C = A * A - 4 * A$ is

$$
\begin{pmatrix}
0 & -1.9688 & -3.9375 & 15.7500 \\
31.5000 & 0 & 0 & -3.9375 \\
15.7500 & 0 & 0 & -1.9688 \\
-15.7500 & 15.7500 & 31.5000 & 0
\end{pmatrix}
$$

Step 2. There are two equal largest values in matrix C, 31.5, where locations are second row and first column, fourth row and third column. In such case, we can identify one of them firstly, or identify both of them simultaneously. To compare the identified results, the following steps identify both elements simultaneously.

Step 3. Draw out all the values in second row and first column, fourth row and third column of pair-wise matrix A, that is

$$
r_2 = \begin{pmatrix} 0.5\ 1\ 2\ 4 \end{pmatrix}, \text{ and } c_1^T = \begin{pmatrix} 1\ 0.5\ 0.25\ 8 \end{pmatrix}
$$

$$r_4 = (8\ 0.25\ 0.5\ 1),\ \text{and}\ c_3^T = (4\ 2\ 1\ 0.5)$$

Step 4. The scalar product b_1 of the vectors r_2 and c_1^T, and the scalar product b_2 of the vectors r_4 and c_3^T in the dimension 4 are

$$b_1 = r_2 \cdot c_1^T = (0.5\ 0.5\ 0.5\ 32)$$

$$b_2 = r_4 \cdot c_3^T = (32\ 0.5\ 0.5\ 0.5)$$

Step 5. The bias identifying vectors f_i $(i = 1, 2)$ are

$$f_1 = b_1 - a_{21} = (0\ 0\ 0\ 31.5)$$

$$f_2 = b_2 - a_{43} = (31.5\ 0\ 0\ 0)$$

Step 6. The values, 31.5, in both bias identifying vectors, are the largest one far from zero, and others are zero in both vectors. The results indicate that $a_{21} = 0.5$ and $a_{43} = 0.5$ are correct while $32 = a_{24}a_{41}$ in b_1 and $32 = a_{41}a_{13}$ in b_2 are the inconsistent elements. Therefore, we identified a_{24}, a_{41} and a_{13} may have problems.

Step 7. As $c_{24} = c_{13} = -3.9375 < 0$ and $c_{41} = -15.75 < 0$, the a_{41} is the largest value far from zero, therefore, the corresponding elements a_{41} is too large, and it is suggested to be decreased. The following is the revising process of a_{41}.

Since $a_{24}a_{41} = 32$ should be equal to $a_{21} = \frac{1}{2}$ in b_1, and we have known $a_{24} = 4$. Therefore, $a_{41} = \frac{a_{21}}{a_{24}} = \frac{1}{8}$. According to reciprocal rule, we can get $a_{14} = 8$. Likewise, Since $a_{41}a_{13} = 32$ should be equal to $a_{43} = \frac{1}{2}$ in b_2, and we have known $a_{13} = 4$. Therefore, $a_{41} = \frac{a_{43}}{a_{13}} = \frac{1}{8}$, and we can get $a_{14} = 8$.

Replace the values of a_{14} and a_{41} in the original comparison matrix A with 8 and 1/8, then the induced bias matrix C becomes a zero matrix as follows, and the modified comparison matrix passed the test with $C.R. = 0 < 0.1$.

$$\begin{pmatrix} 0 & 0 & 0 & 0 \\ 0 & 0 & 0 & 0 \\ 0 & 0 & 0 & 0 \\ 0 & 0 & 0 & 0 \end{pmatrix}$$

Therefore, in such case where there are two or more than two largest values which are equal to each other in the induced bias matrix, we can identify one of them firstly, then use another element to validate the identification result, or identify them simultaneously using the proposed method.

Example 3.3. The 8×8 pair-wise comparison matrix A first introduced in (Kwiesielewicz and Uden 2002) as an example of a pair-wise comparison matrix. This pair-wise matrix is slightly inconsistent with C.R $= 0.1055 > 0.1$.

$$
A = \begin{bmatrix}
1 & 2 & 1/2 & 2 & 1/2 & 2 & 1/2 & 2 \\
1/2 & 1 & 4 & 1 & 1/4 & 1 & 1/4 & 1 \\
2 & 1/4 & 1 & 4 & 1 & 4 & 1 & 4 \\
1/2 & 1 & 1/4 & 1 & 1/4 & 1 & 1/4 & 1 \\
2 & 4 & 1 & 4 & 1 & 4 & 1 & 4 \\
1/2 & 1 & 1/4 & 1 & 1/4 & 1 & 1/4 & 1 \\
2 & 4 & 1 & 4 & 1 & 4 & 1 & 4 \\
1/2 & 1 & 1/4 & 1 & 1/4 & 1 & 1/4 & 1
\end{bmatrix}
$$

According to the proposed method, we have:

Step 1. The induced matrix $C = A * A - 8 * A$ is

$$
\begin{pmatrix}
0 & -1.8750 & 7.5000 & 0 & 0 & 0 & 0 & 0 \\
7.5000 & 0 & -22.5000 & 15.0000 & 3.7500 & 15.0000 & 3.7500 & 15.0000 \\
-1.8750 & 22.5000 & 0 & -3.7500 & -0.9375 & -3.7500 & -0.9375 & -3.7500 \\
0 & -0.9375 & 3.7500 & 0 & 0 & 0 & 0 & 0 \\
0 & -3.7500 & 15.0000 & 0 & 0 & 0 & 0 & 0 \\
0 & -0.9375 & 3.7500 & 0 & 0 & 0 & 0 & 0 \\
0 & -3.7500 & 15.0000 & 0 & 0 & 0 & 0 & 0 \\
0 & -0.9375 & 3.7500 & 0 & 0 & 0 & 0 & 0
\end{pmatrix}
$$

Step 2. The value, 22.5 (third row and second column.), is the largest one in matrix C.

Step 3. The vectors are

$$
r_3 = \begin{pmatrix} 2 & 0.25 & 1 & 4 & 1 & 4 & 1 & 4 \end{pmatrix} \text{ and}
$$

$$
c_2^T = \begin{pmatrix} 2 & 1 & 0.25 & 1 & 4 & 1 & 4 & 1 \end{pmatrix}
$$

Step 4. The scalar product b is

$$
b = r_3 \cdot c_2^T = \begin{pmatrix} 4 & 0.25 & 0.25 & 4 & 4 & 4 & 4 & 4 \end{pmatrix}
$$

Step 5. The bias identifying vector f is

$$
f = b - a_{32} = \begin{pmatrix} 3.75 & 0 & 0 & 3.75 & 3.75 & 3.75 & 3.75 & 3.75 \end{pmatrix}
$$

Step 6. According to the method of minimum, most of the values in bias vector f are deviating equally from zero except two values are equal to zero whose location is the same as a_{32}. Thereby, a_{32} is too small. Likewise, the first $0 = a_{32}a_{22} - a_{32}$, the second $0 = a_{33}a_{32} - a_{32}$. We know that $a_{22} = 1$ and $a_{33} = 1$, so a_{32} is the inconsistent element as there are six elements equally and slightly more than zero. Then step7 is no longer needed. We can also confirm whether a_{32} has problem using the method of order reduction. For instance, removing third row and third column, or second row and second column, we have the following induced matrix:

$$\begin{pmatrix} 0 & 0 & 0 & 0 & 0 & 0 & 0 \\ 0 & 0 & 0 & 0 & 0 & 0 & 0 \\ 0 & 0 & 0 & 0 & 0 & 0 & 0 \\ 0 & 0 & 0 & 0 & 0 & 0 & 0 \\ 0 & 0 & 0 & 0 & 0 & 0 & 0 \\ 0 & 0 & 0 & 0 & 0 & 0 & 0 \\ 0 & 0 & 0 & 0 & 0 & 0 & 0 \end{pmatrix}$$

Increase a_{32} to 4 from 1/4, and a_{23} to 1/4 in the original pair-wise matrix, then the induced matrix C becomes a zero matrix as follows, and the modified comparison matrix passed the test with $C.R. = 0 < 0.1$.

$$\begin{pmatrix} 0 & 0 & 0 & 0 & 0 & 0 & 0 & 0 \\ 0 & 0 & 0 & 0 & 0 & 0 & 0 & 0 \\ 0 & 0 & 0 & 0 & 0 & 0 & 0 & 0 \\ 0 & 0 & 0 & 0 & 0 & 0 & 0 & 0 \\ 0 & 0 & 0 & 0 & 0 & 0 & 0 & 0 \\ 0 & 0 & 0 & 0 & 0 & 0 & 0 & 0 \\ 0 & 0 & 0 & 0 & 0 & 0 & 0 & 0 \\ 0 & 0 & 0 & 0 & 0 & 0 & 0 & 0 \end{pmatrix}$$

The identified inconsistent element is the same as one in (Iida 2009). However, in Iida's method, decision maker has to calculate the number of circular triads with a tie in pair-wise matrix, and eliminate ties from pair-wise matrix to identify the inconsistent element to find the matrix which has a circular triad with lower order and identify the inconsistent element. This identification process is relatively complicated compared with our method.

Example 3.4. In order to demonstrate how the proposed method could identify more than two elements in pair-wise matrix with high order, we generated the following pair-wise matrix by adding one row and one column with random value to the comparison matrix in the second example. The new comparison matrix also denoted by A with $\lambda_{max} = 11.124$ and $C.R. = 0.2328 > 0.1$.

$$A = \begin{bmatrix} 1 & 2 & 1/2 & 2 & 1/2 & 2 & 1/2 & 2 & 1/3 \\ 1/2 & 1 & 4 & 1 & 1/4 & 1 & 1/4 & 1 & 1/4 \\ 2 & 1/4 & 1 & 4 & 1 & 4 & 1 & 4 & 1/7 \\ 1/2 & 1 & 1/4 & 1 & 1/4 & 1 & 1/4 & 1 & 1/6 \\ 2 & 4 & 1 & 4 & 1 & 4 & 1 & 4 & 6 \\ 1/2 & 1 & 1/4 & 1 & 1/4 & 1 & 1/4 & 1 & 1/3 \\ 2 & 4 & 1 & 4 & 1 & 4 & 1 & 4 & 7 \\ 1/2 & 1 & 1/4 & 1 & 1/4 & 1 & 1/4 & 1 & 1/2 \\ 3 & 4 & 7 & 6 & 1/6 & 3 & 1/7 & 2 & 1 \end{bmatrix}$$

According to the proposed inconsistency identification method, we have:

Step 1. The induced matrix $C = A * A - 9 * A$ becomes

$$\begin{pmatrix} 0 & -2.5471 & 9.3333 & 0 & -0.4444 & -1.0000 & -0.4524 & -1.3333 & 6.7381 \\ 7.7500 & 0 & -24.7500 & 15.5000 & 3.5417 & 14.7500 & 3.5357 & 14.5000 & 3.2381 \\ -3.4464 & 22.8214 & 0 & -6.8929 & -1.9137 & -7.3214 & -1.9171 & -7.4643 & 16.7292 \\ 0 & -1.2708 & 4.6667 & 0 & -0.2222 & -0.5000 & -0.2262 & -0.6667 & 3.3690 \\ 16.0000 & 16.2500 & 56.0000 & 32.0000 & 0 & 14.0000 & -0.1429 & 8.0000 & -29.1905 \\ 0.5000 & -0.6042 & 5.8333 & 1.0000 & -0.1944 & 0 & -0.2024 & -0.3333 & 2.0357 \\ 19.0000 & 20.2500 & 63.0000 & 38.0000 & 0.1667 & 17.0000 & 0 & 10.0000 & -37.1905 \\ 1.0000 & 0.0625 & 7.0000 & 2.0000 & -0.1667 & 0.5000 & -0.1786 & 0 & 0.7024 \\ 1.1190 & -8.0119 & -28.4405 & 2.2381 & 11.2262 & 26.2381 & 11.4167 & 34.2381 & 0 \end{pmatrix}$$

Step 2. The largest value, 63, is located at seventh row and third column.

Step 3. The vectors are

$$r_7 = (2 \ 4 \ 1 \ 4 \ 1 \ 4 \ 1 \ 4 \ 7) \text{ and}$$

$$c_3^T = (0.5 \ 4 \ 1 \ 0.25 \ 1 \ 0.25 \ 1 \ 0.25 \ 7)$$

Step 4. The scalar product b is

$$b = r_7 \cdot c_3^T = (1 \ 16 \ 1 \ 1 \ 1 \ 1 \ 1 \ 1 \ 49)$$

Step 5. The bias identifying vector f is

$$f = b - a_{73} = (0 \ 15 \ 0 \ 0 \ 0 \ 0 \ 0 \ 0 \ 48)$$

Step 6. In vectors f and b, we find that all the elements are corresponding to a_{73} except two values are larger than a_{73}. That is, $49 = a_{79}a_{93}$, and $16 = a_{72}a_{23}$. So the decision makers should change the value of a_{23}, a_{72}, a_{79}, and a_{93}.

Furthermore, $c_{23} = -24.75 < 0$ and $c_{72} = 20.25 > 0$. It indicates that a_{23} is too large and a_{72} is too small, so a_{23} should be decreased. Besides, we get $c_{79} = -37.195 < 0$ and $c_{93} = -28.4405 < 0$ from the induced matrix C. Hence, a_{79} and

Table 3.2 The identification process of a_{23}, a_{72}, a_{79}, and a_{93}

Remove	Test	Might problem	Good	Problem
A_3	✓	a_{23}, a_{93}	a_{72}, a_{79}	
A_2	✗	a_{79}, a_{93}	a_{79}	a_{93}
A_7	✗	a_{23}, a_{93}		
A_9	✗	a_{23}, a_{72}	a_{72}	a_{23}

a_{93} may be too large. In Table 3.2, method of matrix order reduction is applied to identify the inconsistency in a_{23}, a_{72}, a_{79}, and a_{93} for their corresponding attributes A_2, A_3, A_7 and A_9 respectively.

The identification process is as follows:

Sub-step 1.   Remove A_3, the order reduced matrix passed test, so a_{72} and a_{79} are consistent while a_{23} and a_{93} might have problem.

Sub-step 2.   Remove A_2, the order reduced matrix could not pass test, so a_{79}, a_{93} might be problematic while a_{79} has been identified to be consistent in Sub-step 1, so a_{93} is one of the inconsistent elements.

Sub-step 3.   Remove A_7, the order reduced matrix could not pass the test, so a_{23}, a_{93} might be problematic while a_{93} has been identified to be inconsistent in Sub-step 2, so continue to check a_{23}.

Sub-step 4.   Remove A_9, the order reduced matrix could not pass the test, so a_{23}, a_{72} might be problematic while a_{72} has been identified to be consistent in Sub-step 1. Hence, the inconsistent element is a_{23}.

Therefore, both a_{23} and a_{93} are the inconsistent elements which have been identified simultaneously.

Adjusting Steps:

$a_{79} = 7$ is consistent while $a_{79}a_{93} = 49$, so we should decrease a_{93} and let $a_{79}a_{93}$ as close to $a_{73} = 1$ as possible. Let us assume $a_{93} = \frac{1}{7}$, and $a_{39} = 7$. Likewise, $a_{72} = 4$ is consistent and $a_{72}a_{23} = 16$, so a_{23} should be decreased and let $a_{72}a_{23}$ as close to $a_{73} = 1$ as possible. Assume $a_{23} = \frac{1}{4}$, and $a_{32} = 4$. Replace the four values from the original comparison matrix A, then the $\lambda_{\max}$ is 9.8491 while the C.R. is 0.0732 less than 0.1, so the consistency test passed, and no correction of judgments is needed. However, as the C.R. is close to 0.1, some elements are still large in the induced matrix. Thus, the decision maker can continue to adjust the value using the proposed method until he gets satisfied result.

Example 3.5. The following 8×8 pair-wise comparison matrix A was first introduced in (Xu and Wei 1999) as an example of an inconsistent pair-wise comparison matrix for the selection of a trucking company, which is based on the performance of the following eight attributes including punctuality, delivery time, temperature control, track and trace, error rate, service reputation, damage loss, and GPS features. This pair-wise matrix is inconsistent with $\lambda_{\max} = 9.669$ and C.R $= 0.169 > 0.1$. This example was also used by Saaty (2003) as an example to describe the method embedded in the *Expert Choice* Software detecting the inconsistencies and also by Cao et al (2008) as an inconsistent pair-wise comparison matrix to test their proposed heuristic approach. We also use this public-domain example to illustrate some special cases in Method for adjusting a_{ij}.

$$
A = \begin{bmatrix}
1 & 5 & 3 & 7 & 6 & 6 & 1/3 & 1/4 \\
1/5 & 1 & 1/3 & 5 & 3 & 3 & 1/5 & 1/7 \\
1/3 & 3 & 1 & 6 & 3 & 4 & 6 & 1/5 \\
1/7 & 1/5 & 1/6 & 1 & 1/3 & 1/4 & 1/7 & 1/8 \\
1/6 & 1/3 & 1/3 & 3 & 1 & 1/2 & 1/5 & 1/6 \\
1/6 & 1/3 & 1/4 & 4 & 2 & 1 & 1/5 & 1/6 \\
3 & 5 & 1/6 & 7 & 5 & 5 & 1 & 1/2 \\
4 & 7 & 5 & 8 & 6 & 6 & 2 & 1
\end{bmatrix}
$$

According to the proposed method, we have:

Step 1. The induced matrix $C = A * A - 8 * A$ is

$$
\begin{pmatrix}
0 & -12.1833 & -10.3611 & 47.3333 & 5.5000 & -1.0833 & 20.9000 & 2.8560 \\
1.7968 & 0 & 1.9310 & -3.0571 & -6.2762 & -10.8595 & 3.0667 & 0.9845 \\
19.4238 & 18.6000 & 0 & 49.9333 & 34.2000 & 21.20000 & -32.6317 & 4.2286 \\
0.2642 & 1.7980 & 0.3177 & 0 & 1.9214 & 2.2548 & 0.5971 & -0.4837 \\
0.9563 & 2.7667 & 0.1028 & -8.4333 & 0 & 3.0833 & 1.7841 & -0.2857 \\
1.3214 & 3.2167 & 1.3111 & -10.9333 & -5.9167 & 0 & 1.7270 & 0.0726 \\
-12.2778 & -6.2667 & 16.2500 & 44.0000 & 18.8333 & 10.9167 & 0 & 1.0393 \\
-11.7905 & 8.6000 & -10.50000 & 101.0000 & 48.6667 & 44.0000 & 24.2762 & 0
\end{pmatrix}
$$

Step 2. The largest value, 101, is located at eight row and fourth column.
Step 3. The vectors are

$$
r_8 = \begin{pmatrix} 4 & 7 & 5 & 8 & 6 & 6 & 2 & 1 \end{pmatrix} \text{ and}
$$

$$
c_4^T = \begin{pmatrix} 7 & 5 & 6 & 1 & 3 & 4 & 7 & 8 \end{pmatrix}
$$

Step 4. The scalar product b is

$$
b = r_8 \cdot c_4^T = \begin{pmatrix} 28 & 35 & 30 & 8 & 18 & 24 & 14 & 8 \end{pmatrix}
$$

Step 5. The bias identifying vector f is

$$
f = b - a_{84} = \begin{pmatrix} 20 & 27 & 22 & 0 & 10 & 16 & 6 & 0 \end{pmatrix}
$$

Step 6. According to the Method for adjusting a_{ij}, there are only two zeroes where the location is fourth and eighth in bias vector f, and others are positive, so a_{84} is too small. However, the value of a_{84} is 8, which is already close to the maximum scale 9, and the other values are larger than zero, which cannot be decreased by increasing the value of a_{84}. In such case, we can remove the fourth attribute or the eighth attribute to test the consistency using the order reduction method. Since the consistency test failed, these two attributes might be consistent. In this case, clearly, the eighth attribute, GPS features with large value are more important than the fourth attribute, track and trace, with small value for the selection of a trucking company.

Therefore, continuing the identification process on the second largest outlier, 49.9333, which is located at third row and fourth column, and repeating Step 3 to Step 6:

Step 3'. The vectors are

$$r_3 = \begin{pmatrix} 0.3333 & 3 & 1 & 6 & 3 & 4 & 6 & 2 \end{pmatrix} \text{ and}$$
$$c_4^T = \begin{pmatrix} 7 & 5 & 6 & 1 & 3 & 4 & 7 & 8 \end{pmatrix}$$

Step 4'. The scalar product b is

$$b = r_3 \cdot c_4^T = \begin{pmatrix} 2.3334 & 15 & 6 & 6 & 9 & 16 & 42 & 1.6 \end{pmatrix}$$

Step 5'. The bias identifying vector f is

$$f = b - a_{34} = \begin{pmatrix} -3.6667 & 9 & 0 & 0 & 3 & 10 & 36 & -4.4 \end{pmatrix}$$

Step 6'. In vectors f and b, most of the elements are around zero, while the number of 36 in vector f is far away zero, which is corresponding to 42 ($a_{37}a_{74}$) in vector b. Hence, the decision makers should check the values of a_{37} and a_{74}.

Furthermore, $c_{37} = -32.6317 < 0$ and $c_{74} = 44 > 0$. It indicates that a_{37} is too large and a_{74} is too small, so the value of a_{37} should be decreased. The inconsistent element in the pair-wise comparison matrix has been identified.

In order to validate that the inconsistent element is a_{37}, we removed third attribute and seventh attribute respectively to test the consistency. Both consistency tests passed. Therefore, the inconsistent element is a_{37}. Since $a_{37}a_{74}$ is supposed to be equal to 6, hence we can get $a_{37} = 6/a_{74} = 6/7 = 0.86$. Either 0.5 or 1 in the 9-point scale could be selected as the optimal value of this inconsistent entry. Assume $a_{37} = \frac{1}{2}$, and $a_{73} = 2$. Replace these two values in the original pair-wise comparison matrix with the above values and test the consistency, the consistency test passed with $\lambda_{max} = 8.8117$ and $C.R. = 0.0828 < 0.1$.

Comparisons have been made among the proposed method, Xu and Wei' method, Saaty's method and Cao's et al method. In Xu and Wei (1999), a consistent matrix by an auto-adaptive process based on the original inconsistent matrix was proposed instead of revising single elements. For instance, the element a_{ij} in the original inconsistent comparison matrix is replaced by $b_{ij} = a_{ij}^{\lambda} (w_i/w_j)^{1-\lambda}$, and $0 < \lambda < 1$, where w_i and w_j are the priority vector derived from the original inconsistent matrix. Thus, a new consistent matrix $B = (b_{ij})$ was generated by adjusting the parameter λ repeatedly, and the decision makers use this new matrix as a reference for revising the original inconsistent matrix instead of the original comparison matrix. Therefore, Xu and Wei's method lost some original comparison information and made some perturbations when adjusting the parameter λ. Clearly, the more bias values of elements are zeros or close to zero, the more original matrix information will be preserved in the bias matrix between the modified comparison matrix and the original comparison matrix. The bias matrix can be calculated by subtracting the modified comparison matrix from the original comparison matrix. For example, in Xu and Wei's (1999) final modified comparison matrix, when the parameter $\lambda = 0.98$, the bias matrix becomes:

$$\begin{pmatrix} 0 & 0.4760 & 0.6610 & -0.5230 & 0.1120 & 0.3140 & -0.0917 & -0.0420 \\ -0.0210 & 0 & 0.0073 & 0.4840 & 0.3290 & 0.4200 & -0.0220 & -0.0041 \\ -0.0937 & -0.0670 & 0 & -0.7490 & -0.4600 & -0.1880 & 1.8450 & -0.0490 \\ 0.0099 & -0.0210 & 0.0187 & 0 & -0.0397 & -0.0370 & 0.0089 & 0.0210 \\ -0.0033 & -0.0407 & 0.0443 & 0.3190 & 0 & -0.0610 & 0.0030 & 0.0197 \\ -0.0093 & -0.0547 & -0.0160 & 0.5210 & 0.2160 & 0 & -0.0040 & 0.137 \\ 0.6460 & 0.5030 & -0.0743 & -0.4790 & -0.0730 & 0.1010 & 0 & -0.0010 \\ 0.5810 & 0.2140 & 0.9760 & -1.6240 & -0.7830 & -0.5510 & 0.0040 & 0 \end{pmatrix}$$

In the bias matrix, there are some relatively larger perturbations such as a_{37}, a_{84}, a_{83}, a_{34}, a_{14} and etc. Many values in the original matrix have been changed. For example, the value of a_{84} is 12.339 and 9.624 for $\lambda = 0.5$ and $\lambda = 0.98$ respectively in the modified pair-wise comparison matrix, which are higher than the maximum scale 9 (Saaty 1980).

Likewise, in Cao et al (2008), the consistent matrix based on the original inconsistent matrix is automatically generated instead of revising single element. The deviation of the generated pair-wise comparison information in inconsistent matrix is expressed as a deviation matrix. The consistency ratio is improved by an iterative process which adjusts the deviation matrix. Although the consistency test passed with $C.R. = 0.0997 < 0.1$, and they illustrated that their proposed method could retain more original comparison information than Xu and Wei's method did, their method also made some perturbations when adjusting the parameter γ. The following bias matrix is calculated by subtracting the modified comparison matrix when the parameter $\gamma = 0.98$ from the original comparison matrix.

$$\begin{pmatrix} 0 & 0.5588 & 0.6318 & -0.6743 & 0.1441 & 0.3921 & -0.0868 & -0.0468 \\ -0.0252 & 0 & 0.0123 & 0.5776 & 0.3825 & 0.4608 & -0.0268 & -0.0057 \\ -0.0890 & -0.1151 & 0 & -0.9149 & -0.5351 & -0.2774 & 1.4895 & -0.0487 \\ 0.0126 & -0.0261 & 0.0504 & 0 & -0.0472 & -0.0427 & 0.0116 & 0.0220 \\ -0.0041 & -0.0487 & 0.0162 & 0.3772 & 0 & -0.0722 & 0.0040 & 0.0223 \\ -0.0116 & -0.0605 & 0.0285 & 0.5834 & 0.2522 & 0 & -0.0055 & 0.0173 \\ 0.6196 & 0.5901 & -0.0550 & -0.6136 & -0.1012 & 0.1339 & 0 & -0.0004 \\ 0.6311 & 0.2707 & 0.9785 & -1.7130 & -0.9235 & -0.6949 & 0.0016 & 0 \end{pmatrix}$$

In the above bias matrix, there are also some relatively larger perturbations such as a_{84}, a_{37}, a_{83}, a_{85}, a_{34} and etc. Besides, some values of elements in the original matrix had been changed undesirably. For instance, $a_{84} = 11.2647$ for $\gamma = 0.5$, and $a_{84} = 9.7130$ for $\gamma = 0.98$ in the modified pair-wise comparison matrix, which are higher than the maximum scale 9 (Saaty 1980).

In addition to the above two methods, a similar matrix $\varepsilon_{ij} = a_{ij} (w_j/w_i)$ is constructed to identify the most inconsistent element in the inconsistency identification method embedded of the AHP software *Expert Choice*. The above comparison matrix A was also introduced by Saaty (2003) as an example (Saaty's method in the following). The inconsistent element a_{37} is identified by Saaty's method, and replaced with the value of $w_i/w_j = 1/2$. Compared with the other two methods, Saaty's method is the easier to use as it is based on the ratio of priorities and designed for the Perron Eigenvalue Method (EM) (Saaty 1977) and AHP. However, the 'precise' number recommended by Saaty's method is $a_{ij} = \omega_i/\omega_j$, which is an approximated value since the ω_i and ω_j can be calculated by the different method to derive priority vectors. In the example described by Saaty (2003), the method gives the 'precise' value 1/2 by approximating the $a_{37} = \omega_3/\omega_7 = 1/2.18 \approx 1/2$ to adjust the a_{37} and a_{73}. When we select the following pairs, (1,1), (1/3,3), (1/4,4), (1/5,5), (1/6,6) and (1/7,7) to approximate the pairs (a_{37}, a_{73}), we get the following CRs: 0.0886,0.084,0.086,0.0897,0.093, 0.097, respectively. All consistency ratios are less than 0.1, the priority vector derived by replacing one of the pairs of values are acceptable in the AHP, however, the result will be unacceptable in the ANP. The 'precise' value is no longer precise in the ANP, and it is necessary to show the modification direction and provide some optimal values for the decision makers.

To summarize, the formula used by Xu and Wei's method, Saaty's method and Cao's et al method are $\varepsilon_{ij} = a_{ij} (w_j/w_i)$, $b_{ij} = a_{ij}^{\lambda} (w_i/w_j)^{1-\lambda}$ and $d_{ij}' = \gamma a_{ij}/(w_i/w_j) + (1 - \gamma)$, respectively. All three methods are based on the priority vector ratios, which are calculated by the inconsistent comparison matrix. As reviewed in introductory part, different methods, other than the EM, have been proposed to derive a priority vector with a given positive reciprocal matrix A. Different methods may yield different vectors (ω_i, ω_j). The inconsistent entries and the approximated value ω_i/ω_j of the identified inconsistent entry a_{ij} may be different when different methods are selected to calculate ω_i, ω_j.

In the proposed method, the inconsistent element a_{37} is identified by the induced matrix C, which is only based on the original comparison matrix A. The decision maker only needs to adjust a_{37} and a_{73} without changing other elements. After identifying the inconsistent entry, one can use any of the known methods to derive the priority vector. It is more practical and keeps most of the information provided by the original comparison matrix. For instance, as identified above, either 0.5 or 1 in the 9-point scale could be selected as the optimal value of this inconsistent entry a_{37}. Let $a_{37} = \frac{1}{2}$, and $a_{73} = 2$, and the modified comparison matrix could be generated by replacing these two values in the original comparison matrix. Thus, the bias matrix becomes:

$$\begin{pmatrix} 0 & 0 & 0 & 0 & 0 & 0 & 0 & 0 \\ 0 & 0 & 0 & 0 & 0 & 0 & 0 & 0 \\ 0 & 0 & 0 & 0 & 0 & 0 & 5.5000 & 0 \\ 0 & 0 & 0 & 0 & 0 & 0 & 0 & 0 \\ 0 & 0 & 0 & 0 & 0 & 0 & 0 & 0 \\ 0 & 0 & -1.8333 & 0 & 0 & 0 & 0 & 0 \\ 0 & 0 & 0 & 0 & 0 & 0 & 0 & 0 \\ 0 & 0 & 0 & 0 & 0 & 0 & 0 & 0 \end{pmatrix}$$

All values provided by experts in the original comparison matrix have been retained except the inconsistent elements a_{37} and a_{73}. Furthermore, the proposed method does not violate the scale [1, 9], needs fewer computations than Xu and Wei' method and Cao's et al method, and also preserve more original comparison information than these two methods. Compare with Saaty's method, the proposed method is based on only the original comparison matrix A instead of the ratio of priorities. Any of the known methods, such as EM, DLSM, WLSM, LLSM/GMS, and GPM, could be applied to derive the priority vectors for the revised reciprocal comparison matrix by the proposed method and the same inconsistent entries will always be identified. Furthermore, the proposed method can also show the modification direction and provide the optimal values.

3.3.2 Illustrative Examples for Fast Inconsistency Identification and Adjustment Method

The *Example 3.2* and *Example 3.3* introduced above are used in this study as *Example 3.6* and *Example 3.7*, respectively, to demonstrate the proposed fast inconsistency identification method.

Example 3.6. The induced bias matrix C, computed by the proposed IBM method in above *Example 3.2* is,

$$\begin{pmatrix} 0 & -1.9688 & -3.9375 & 15.7500 \\ 31.5000 & 0 & 0 & -3.9375 \\ 15.7500 & 0 & 0 & -1.9688 \\ -15.7500 & 15.7500 & 31.5000 & 0 \end{pmatrix}$$

It can easily be observed that there are only two non-zero rows (first and fourth), and two non-zero columns (first and fourth) in the IBM, which is identical to the formula (3.53). In addition, there is only one sign different from those elements whether located at first and fourth rows or columns. Therefore, according to the principle of above proposed fast inconsistency identification method, the inconsistent elements are a_{14} and a_{41}. Besides, since $c_{14} = 15.75 > 0$, a_{14} is too small and should be increased. According to the revising formula (3.55) of a_{ip}, we get

$$a_{14} = \frac{1}{4-2} \sum_{k=2}^{3} a_{1k} a_{k4} = \frac{1}{2} (2 \times 4 + 4 \times 2) = 8, \quad a_{41} = \frac{1}{a_{14}} = \frac{1}{8}$$

The identified inconsistent element and its revised result are the same as shown in above *Example 3.2*.

Example 3.7. The induced bias matrix C, computed by the proposed IBMM in above *Example 3.3*, is showed below.

$$
\begin{pmatrix}
0 & -1.8750 & 7.5000 & 0 & 0 & 0 & 0 & 0 \\
7.5000 & 0 & -22.5000 & 15.0000 & 3.7500 & 15.0000 & 3.7500 & 15.0000 \\
-1.8750 & 22.5000 & 0 & -3.7500 & -0.9375 & -3.7500 & -0.9375 & -3.7500 \\
0 & -0.9375 & 3.7500 & 0 & 0 & 0 & 0 & 0 \\
0 & -3.7500 & 15.0000 & 0 & 0 & 0 & 0 & 0 \\
0 & -0.9375 & 3.7500 & 0 & 0 & 0 & 0 & 0 \\
0 & -3.7500 & 15.0000 & 0 & 0 & 0 & 0 & 0 \\
0 & -0.9375 & 3.7500 & 0 & 0 & 0 & 0 & 0
\end{pmatrix}
$$

It can easily be observed that there are only two non-zero rows (second and third), and two non-zero columns (second and third) in above IBM. Likewise, there is only one sign different from those elements whether located at second and third rows or columns. Both are identical to the formula (3.53). Therefore, according to the above fast identification method, the inconsistent elements are a_{23} and a_{32}. Besides, since $c_{23} = -22.5 < 0$ and $c_{32} = 22.5 > 0$, we can get that a_{23} is too large, and a_{32} is too small.

Since $c_{23} = \sum_{k=1}^{8} a_{2k} a_{k3} - 8 a_{23} = \sum_{k=1, \neq 2,3}^{8} a_{2k} a_{k3} + a_{22} a_{23} + a_{23} a_{33} - 8 a_{23}$,

assume $c_{23} = 0$, $a_{23} = \frac{1}{6} \sum_{k=1, \neq 2,3}^{8} a_{2k} a_{k3} = \frac{1}{6} (\frac{1}{2} \times \frac{1}{2} + 1 \times \frac{1}{4} + \frac{1}{4} \times 1 + 1 \times \frac{1}{4} + \frac{1}{4}$

$\times 1 + 1 \times \frac{1}{4}) = \frac{1}{4}$, and $c_{32} = 4$. For simplicity, since a_{23} is inconsistent, assume $a_{2k} a_{k3} = a'_{23}$, $(k = 1, 4, 5, 6, 7, 8)$, we can use a'_{23} to be the value of a_{23} in order to let it be consistent. Clearly, any value of pair of $a_{2k} a_{k3} = a'_{23}$ $(k = 1, 4, 5, 6, 7, 8)$ is $\frac{1}{4}$, which is the same as shown in above *Example 3.3*.

The above examples show that the inconsistent elements can be determined by observing and analyzing the non-zero row (column), and sign identification of the bias elements in the IBM C instead of following the above proposed seven steps of inconsistency identification. Therefore, the proposed method is simpler and faster than the previous method for the special case with only one pair of inconsistent elements in the original PCM.

References

Bozóki S, Fülöp J, Poesz A (2011) On pairwise comparison matrices that can be made consistent by the modification of a few elements. Cent Eur J Oper Res 19:157–175

Cao D, Leung LC, Law JS (2008) Modifying inconsistent comparison matrix in analytic hierarchy process: a heuristic approach. Decis Supp Syst 44:944–953

Ergu D, Kou G (2011) Questionnaire design improvement and missing item scores estimation for rapid and efficient decision making. Ann Oper Res 2011. doi:10.1007/s10479-011-0922-3

Ergu D, Kou G, Peng Y, Shi Y (2011b) A simple method to improve the consistency ratio of the pair-wise comparison matrix in ANP. Eur J Oper Res 213(1):246–259. doi:10.1016/j.ejor.2011.03.014

Ergu D, Kou G, Peng Y, Shi Y, Shi Yu (2011c) BIMM: a bias induced matrix model for incomplete reciprocal pairwise comparison matrix. J Multi-Crit Decis Anal. doi:10.1002/mcda.472

Ergu D, Kou G, Peng Y, Shi Y, Shi Yu (2011d) The analytic hierarchy process: task scheduling and resource allocation in cloud computing environment. J Supercomput. doi:10.1007/s11227-011-0625-1

Ergu D, Kou G, Shi Y, Shi Yu (2011e) Analytic network process in risk assessment and decision analysis. Comput Oper Res. doi:10.1016/j.cor.2011.03.005

Ergu D, Kou G, Peng Y, Shi Y (2011f) Further discussions on "A simple method to improve the consistency ratio of the pair-wise comparison matrix in ANP". Working paper, 2011

Iida Y (2009) Ordinality consistency test about items and notation of a pairwise comparison matrix in AHP. In: Proceedings of the international symposium on the Analytic Hierarchy Process

Kwiesielewicz M, Uden E (2002) Problem of inconsistent and contradictory judgements in pairwise comparison method in sense of AHP. In: Sloot PMA et al. (eds) Computational science – ICCS 2002, Lecture notes in computer science 2329, pp 468–473

Liu W (1999) A new method of rectifying judgment matrix. Syst Eng Theory Pract 6:30–34, in Chinese

Saaty TL (1977) A scaling method for priorities in hierarchical structures. J Math Psychol 15(3):234–281

Saaty TL (1980) The analytical hierarchy process. McGraw-Hill, New York

Saaty TL (1991) Some mathematical concepts of the analytic hierarchy process. Behaviormetrika 29:1–9

Saaty TL (2001b) Deriving the AHP 1–9 scale from first principles. In: ISAHP 2001 proceedings, Bern, Switzerland

Saaty TL (2003) Decision-making with the AHP: why is the principal eigenvector necessary. Eur J Oper Res 145(1):85–89

Xu Z, Wei C (1999) A consistency improving method in the analytic hierarchy process. Eur J Oper Res 116:443–449

Chapter 4
IBMM for Missing Data Estimation

In Chap. 3, the induced bias matrix is proposed to identify the inconsistent elements in a complete pairwise comparison matrix (PCM). Besides inconsistency, a PCM may be incomplete due to limited expertise or unwillingness to judge. For an incomplete pairwise comparison matrix (IPCM), the missing values must first be estimated in order for the IPCM to be useful. The revised PCM needs to pass the consistency test. For this purpose, we have extended the IBMM to estimate the missing values in an IPCM (Ergu et al. 2011c). The revised PCM with the estimated values by IBMM is shown to satisfy the consistency requirement. In this Chapter, the details of IBMM for missing data estimation in AHP/ANP are comprehensively addressed.

4.1 Basics of the IBMM for Missing Data Estimation

For an incomplete pairwise comparison matrix (IPCM) with some missing values, the corresponding revised PCM should also follow the *Theorems* and *Corollaries* of IBMM, that is, if we fill in the missing values with the unknown variables (denoted by x, $1/x$; y, $1/y$; z, $1/z$; ...), then the revised 'complete' pairwise comparison (RCM) should also follow the *Theorems* of IBMM previously stated in Chap. 3. Therefore, the proposed IBMM method can not only estimate the corresponding missing values, but also maintain the revised pairwise comparison matrix consistency.

In an incomplete pairwise comparison matrix (IPCM), there are $2p$ unknown entries if p comparisons are missing due to its reciprocity. To estimate the missing entries in an IPCM, firstly fill in the missing entries with the variables denoted by x, y, z etc. and the corresponding reciprocal values with unknown variables to get the revised 'complete' PCM, also denoted by A, then the following corresponding theorem and corollaries can be derived based on the *Theorem 3.1, Corollary 3.1, Corollary 3.2 and Corollary 3.3*:

Theorem 4.1. *The induced bias matrix $C = AA - nA$ should be a zero matrix if the revised pairwise comparison matrix (PCM) A of the IPCM is perfectly consistent.*

Corollary 4.1. *The induced bias matrix $C = AA - nA$ should be as close as possible to zero matrix if the revised pairwise comparison matrix (PCM) A of the IPCM is approximately consistent.*

Corollary 4.2. *The induced bias matrix $C = AA - nA$ must not be a zero matrix if the revised pairwise comparison matrix (PCM) A of the IPCM is inconsistent, and there must be some inconsistent entries in the induced bias matrix C deviating far away from zero*

Corollary 4.3. *All entries in the main diagonal of the induced bias matrix $C = AA - nA$ should be zeroes as long as the revised pairwise comparison matrix (PCM) A of the incomplete PCM the comparison matrix is satisfied with the reciprocal condition no matter it is consistent or not.*

Based on the above *Theorem* and *Corollaries*, we can derive the following theorem.

The Theorem of the Induced Bias Matrix Model (IBMM):

The induced bias matrix $C = AA - nA$ should be equal (or close) to a zero matrix if the revised PCM is perfectly (or approximately) consistent. That is

$$C = AA - nA \begin{cases} = 0 & \text{if } a_{ik}a_{kj} = a_{ij} \\ \approx 0 & \text{if } a_{ik}a_{kj} \approx a_{ij} \end{cases}$$

where A is the revised 'complete' PCM after replacing the missing values in the IPCM with unknown variables x, $1/x$, y, $1/y$, z, $1/z$, etc. The n denotes the order of PCM.

It can be seen from the *Theorem* of IBMM for estimating the missing values, the following two conditions hold:

1. All the entries of the induced bias matrix $C = AA - nA$ should be equal to zeroes if the revised pairwise comparison matrix A is perfectly consistent.
2. Most of the entries of the induced bias matrix $C = AA - nA$ should be close to zeroes if the revised pairwise comparison matrix A is approximately consistent.

Thus, for the revised 'complete' PCM, the unknown variables can be estimated by minimizing the values of the induced bias matrix, namely, solving the corresponding equations generated from the induced bias matrix. The steps necessary to estimate the missing values are presented next.

4.2   The Processes of Estimating Missing Data by the IBMM

Based on the *Theorem* of IBMM aforementioned, to make the revised pairwise comparison matrix completely consistent or approximately consistent, we need to minimize the bias values with unknown variables of the induced bias matrix C to

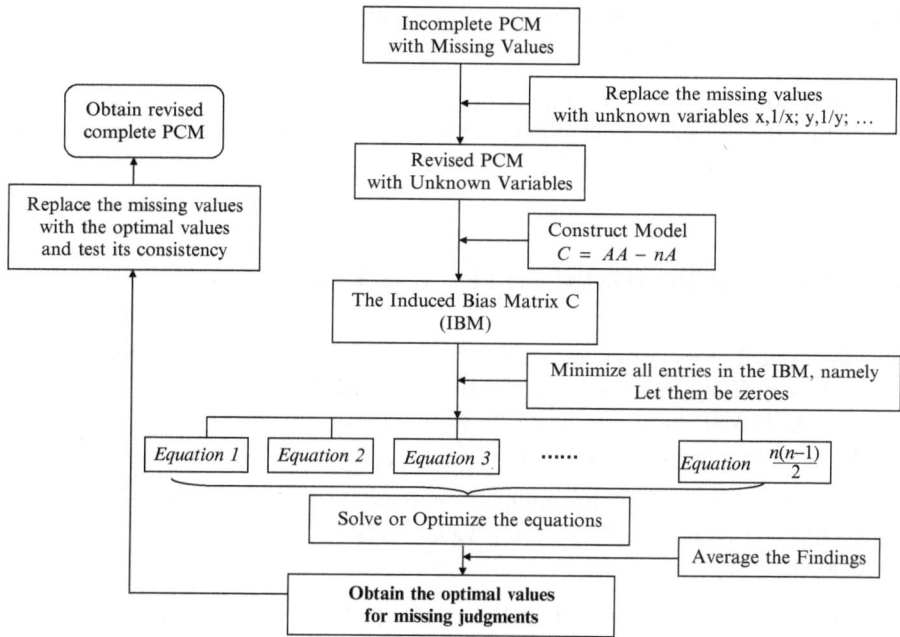

Fig. 4.1 The IBMM for estimating the missing entries in IPCM

be zeroes or close to zeroes, then there are some corresponding systems of linear or nonlinear equations that hold. Solving the system of linear or nonlinear equations generated from the upper triangular matrix or the lower triangular matrix to find or estimate the missing value(s) by averaging all solutions of the equations. Hence, how to estimate the missing values while keeping the revised PCM consistency becomes how to solve or optimize the corresponding systems of linear or nonlinear equations.

The structure of the proposed model (IBMM) for estimating the missing data in AHP/ANP is showed in Fig. 4.1.

Therefore, the steps of the IBMM for estimating the missing values can be summarized as:

Step 1: Replace the missing values with unknown variables x,1/x; y,1/y; z,1/z etc. for the IRPCM and get the revised 'complete' PCM A.

Step 2: Construct the proposed model $C = AA - nA$ and calculate the induced bias matrix C.

Step 3: Minimize all bias entries of the induced bias matrix C, that is, let all entries with unknown variables be (equal to) zeros, and get $n(n-1)/2$ number of equations.

Step 4: Solve these linear or nonlinear equations.

Step 5: Average all solutions in order to keep the global consistency and find the optimal values of variables.

Step 6: Replace the missing values with the optimal values and test the consistency for the revised PCM in order to maintain its consistency.

Before some numerical examples are used to illustrate the proposed IBMM for estimating the missing values, the general incomplete PCM in order three is first used to prove the correctness of the proposed method next.

4.3 Proofs of the IBMM for IPCM in Order Three

The theoretical proofs of the proposed IBMM for inconsistency identification have been made in Chap. 3. In addition, the basics of IBMM for estimating the missing data in AHP/ANP have also been proposed above. To demonstrate this model, without loss of generality, let us first analyze a general IPCM in two cases:

Case-1: Introduce one missing comparison to the IPCM, without loss of generality, assume a_{12} and a_{21} is the missing values. Then follow the above steps of the IBMM.

Step 1: Let $a_{12} = \frac{1}{x}$, $a_{21} = x$, then the revised pairwise comparison matrix (PCM) A with unknown variable x is

$$
\begin{pmatrix}
a_{11} & \frac{1}{x} & a_{13} \\
x & a_{22} & a_{23} \\
a_{31} & a_{32} & a_{33}
\end{pmatrix}
\tag{4.1}
$$

Step 2: Construct the proposed model $C = AA - nA$, and then the induced bias matrix C is

$$
\begin{pmatrix}
0 & \frac{a_{11}}{x} + \frac{a_{22}}{x} + a_{13}a_{32} - \frac{3}{x} & a_{11}a_{13} + \frac{a_{23}}{x} + a_{13}a_{33} - 3a_{13} \\
xa_{11} + xa_{22} + a_{23}a_{31} - 3x & 0 & xa_{13} + a_{22}a_{23} + a_{23}a_{33} - 3a_{23} \\
a_{31}a_{11} + xa_{32} + a_{33}a_{31} - 3a_{31} & \frac{a_{31}}{x} + a_{32}a_{22} + a_{33}a_{32} - 3a_{32} & 0
\end{pmatrix}
\tag{4.2}
$$

Step 3: Minimize all bias entries of the induced bias matrix C, that is, let all entries with unknown variables equal to zeros, and get six equations:
The system of linear equations generated from the upper triangular matrix:

$$
\begin{cases}
\dfrac{a_{11}}{x} + \dfrac{a_{22}}{x} + ya_{32} - \dfrac{3}{x} = 0 \\[2mm]
ya_{11} + \dfrac{a_{23}}{x} + ya_{33} - 3y = 0 \\[2mm]
xy + a_{22}a_{23} + a_{32}a_{33} - 3a_{23} = 0
\end{cases}
\tag{4.3}
$$

The system of linear equations generated from the lower triangular matrix is

$$
\begin{cases}
xa_{11} + xa_{22} + a_{23}a_{31} - 3x = 0 \\
a_{31}a_{11} + xa_{32} + a_{33}a_{31} - 3a_{31} = 0 \\
\dfrac{a_{31}}{x} + a_{32}a_{22} + a_{33}a_{32} - 3a_{32} = 0
\end{cases}
\tag{4.4}
$$

Step 4: Solve one of these two systems of linear equations to find the unknown variable x. In this example, the solution of the variable x can be found by solving only one of the equations. For instance, solve the third equation in (4.3) or the second equation in (4.4) in above two systems of linear equations (because there is only one missing value) and we can find

$$
x = a_{23}a_{31} = \frac{1}{a_{32}}a_{31} = a_{23}\frac{1}{a_{13}} = a_{21}
\tag{4.5}
$$

The result is consistent with the above assumption, which is also accordance with the consistency condition $a_{ik}a_{kj} = a_{ij}$ for all i, j and k.

Because the solution is singular and consistent with the assumption, hence, the Step 5 and Step 6 are skipped.

Case-2: Introduce two missing comparisons to the general 3×3 IPCM A, without loss of generality, assume a_{12} and a_{21}, a_{13} and a_{31} are the missing values. Then follow the above steps of the IBMM.

Step 1: Assume $a_{12} = \frac{1}{x}$, $a_{21} = x$ and $a_{13} = y$, $a_{31} = \frac{1}{y}$, then the revised reciprocal pairwise comparison matrix (RPCM) A with unknown variables x and y is

$$
\begin{pmatrix}
a_{11} & \frac{1}{x} & y \\
x & a_{22} & a_{23} \\
\frac{1}{y} & a_{32} & a_{33}
\end{pmatrix}
\tag{4.6}
$$

Step 2: Construct the model $C = AA - nA$, and then the induced bias matrix C is

$$
C = \begin{pmatrix}
0 & \frac{a_{11}}{x} + \frac{a_{22}}{x} + ya_{32} - \frac{3}{x} & ya_{11} + \frac{a_{23}}{x} + ya_{33} - 3y \\
xa_{11} + xa_{22} + \frac{a_{23}}{y} - 3x & 0 & xy + a_{22}a_{23} + a_{32}a_{33} - 3a_{23} \\
\frac{a_{11}}{y} + xa_{32} + \frac{a_{33}}{y} - \frac{3}{y} & \frac{1}{xy} + a_{32}a_{22} + a_{33}a_{32} - 3a_{32} & 0
\end{pmatrix}
$$

Step 3: Minimize all bias entries of the induced bias matrix C, that is, let all entries with unknown variables be (equal to) zeros, and then the following equations hold:

System of equations generated from the upper triangular entries

$$
\begin{cases}
\dfrac{a_{11}}{x} + \dfrac{a_{22}}{x} + ya_{32} - \dfrac{3}{x} = 0 \\[2mm]
ya_{11} + \dfrac{a_{23}}{x} + ya_{33} - 3y = 0 \\[2mm]
xy + a_{22}a_{23} + a_{32}a_{33} - 3a_{23} = 0
\end{cases}
\tag{4.7}
$$

System of equations generated from the lower triangular entries

$$
\begin{cases}
xa_{11} + xa_{22} + \dfrac{a_{23}}{y} - 3x = 0 \\[2mm]
\dfrac{a_{11}}{y} + xa_{32} + \dfrac{a_{33}}{y} - \dfrac{3}{y} = 0 \\[2mm]
\dfrac{1}{xy} + a_{32}a_{22} + a_{33}a_{32} - 3a_{32} = 0
\end{cases}
\tag{4.8}
$$

Step 4: Solve one of the above two systems of equations, then the relationship of the variables (missing values) x and y can be found.

$$
xy = \frac{1}{a_{32}} = a_{23}
\tag{4.9}
$$

If $x = a_{21}$, then $y = \frac{a_{23}}{a_{21}} = a_{12}a_{23} = a_{13}$. The result is consistent with above assumption.

In an $n \times n$ reciprocal PCM, only $n(n-1)/2$ comparisons are required to complete the reciprocal PCM in the upper diagonal triangular matrix. The entries in the lower diagonal triangular matrix are the reciprocal values of the corresponding entries given by experts in the upper diagonal triangular matrix. In order to make a valid decision, the $n(n-1)/$ comparisons should be completed for an n-by-n PCM. If the PCM contains some missing comparisons, obviously, the less the missing comparisons are, the more reliable the decision will be. An n-by-n incomplete reciprocal PCM contains $2p$ missing entries if p comparisons are missing in the IPCM. If $p > n(n-1)/4$, the explicit solutions cannot be found for the proposed IBMM and the missing values cannot be estimated by the IBMM. In this example, as $n = 3$, we need three valid comparisons. However, there is only one valid comparison for PCM, and two required comparisons are missing. This means the information provided by experts is not enough to make a valid decision because the number of valid comparisons is less than the number of the missing comparisons, which is already more than the required number of the IBMM to find explicit solution $(p \le n(n-1)/4 = 1.5)$, hence, the IBMM could not estimate the missing values in the PCM.

4.4 Illustrative Examples

4.4.1 Illustrative Examples in Order Three

In the above section, we have proved two cases for a general 3×3 incomplete PCM A with one and two missing comparisons respectively. In order to illustrate the above two cases, two corresponding concrete numerical incomplete 3×3 PCM are introduced below.

Example 4.1. Assume a complete reciprocal pairwise comparison matrix with $(\lambda_{\max} = 3)$ and $CR = 0$ be

$$
\begin{pmatrix}
1 & 3 & 6 \\
\frac{1}{3} & 1 & 2 \\
\frac{1}{6} & \frac{1}{2} & 1
\end{pmatrix}
$$

Then assume the $a_{23} = 2$ is the missing value, namely the corresponding incomplete PCM is

$$
\begin{pmatrix}
1 & 3 & 6 \\
\frac{1}{3} & 1 & \times \\
\frac{1}{6} & \times & 1
\end{pmatrix}
$$

Then follow the steps of the IBMM to find the missing value.

Step 1: Assume $a_{23} = x, a_{32} = \frac{1}{x}$, then the revised PCM A with unknown variables x becomes

$$
\begin{pmatrix}
1 & 3 & 6 \\
\frac{1}{3} & 1 & x \\
\frac{1}{6} & \frac{1}{x} & 1
\end{pmatrix}
$$

Step 2: The induced bias matrix $C = AA - nA$ is

$$
\begin{pmatrix}
0 & -3 + \frac{6}{x} & -6 + 3x \\
-\frac{1}{3} + \frac{x}{6} & 0 & 2 - x \\
-\frac{1}{6} + \frac{1}{3x} & \frac{1}{2} - \frac{1}{x} & 0
\end{pmatrix}
$$

Step 3: Minimize all bias entries of the induced bias matrix C, that is, let all entries with unknown variables equal to zeros, and then the following equations hold: System of equations generated from the upper triangular entries

$$
\begin{cases}
-3 + \frac{6}{x} = 0 \\
-6 + 3x = 0 \\
2 - x = 0
\end{cases}
$$

System of equations generated from the lower triangular entries

$$
\begin{cases}
-\frac{1}{3} + \frac{x}{6} = 0 \\
-\frac{1}{6} + \frac{1}{3x} = 0 \\
\frac{1}{2} - \frac{1}{x} = 0
\end{cases}
$$

Step 4: Solve one of the above two systems of equations, then the variable x can be found.

$$x = 2$$

The result is consistent with the missing value. Therefore, Step 5 and Step 6 are skipped.

Example 4.2. Introduce two missing comparisons to the above given 3×3 matrix, then it contains four missing values. Assume the $a_{13} = 6$ and $a_{23} = 2$ are the two missing comparisons, namely, the corresponding incomplete PCM is

$$
\begin{pmatrix}
1 & 3 & \times \\
\frac{1}{3} & 1 & \times \\
\times & \times & 1
\end{pmatrix}
$$

Then follow the steps of the IBMM to estimate the missing values.

Step 1: Assume $a_{13} = y, a_{31} = \frac{1}{y}$, and $a_{23} = x, a_{31} = \frac{1}{x}$, then the revised pairwise comparison matrix (PCM) A with unknown variables x and y becomes

$$
\begin{pmatrix}
1 & 3 & y \\
\frac{1}{3} & 1 & x \\
\frac{1}{y} & \frac{1}{x} & 1
\end{pmatrix}
$$

Step 2: The induced bias matrix $C = AA - nA$ is

$$
\begin{pmatrix}
0 & -3 + \frac{y}{x} & -y + 3x \\
-\frac{1}{3} + \frac{x}{y} & 0 & \frac{y}{3} - x \\
-\frac{1}{y} + \frac{1}{3x} & \frac{3}{y} - \frac{1}{x} & 0
\end{pmatrix}
$$

Step 3: Minimize all bias entries of the induced bias matrix C, that is, let all entries with unknown variables be equal to zeros, and then the following equations hold: System of equations generated from the upper triangular entries

$$
\begin{cases}
-3 + \frac{y}{x} = 0 \\
-y + 3x = 0 \\
\frac{y}{3} - x = 0
\end{cases}
$$

System of equations generated from the lower triangular entries

$$\begin{cases} -\frac{1}{3} + \frac{x}{y} = 0 \\ -\frac{1}{y} + \frac{1}{3x} = 0 \\ \frac{3}{y} - \frac{1}{x} = 0 \end{cases}$$

Step 4: Solve one of the above two systems of equations, then the relationship of two unknown variables x and y can be solved below:

$$y = 3x$$

If $x = 2$, then $y = 6$. The result is consistent with the missing value assumed above. Therefore, Step 5 and Step 6 are skipped here. It also shows that the PCM is becoming an artificial PCM if there are not enough valid entries in PCM.

4.4.2 Illustrative Examples in Order Four

In order to expand the proposed IBMM to the incomplete PCM with higher order, the following example is used to illustrate the proposed IBMM.

Example 4.3. Assume a 4×4 complete PCM with $\lambda_{max} = 4.0076$ and $CR = 0.00284$ be

$$\begin{pmatrix} 1 & \frac{1}{9} & \frac{1}{2} & \frac{1}{5} \\ 9 & 1 & 5 & 2 \\ 2 & \frac{1}{5} & 1 & \frac{1}{2} \\ 5 & \frac{1}{2} & 2 & 1 \end{pmatrix}$$

Without loss of generality, let us assume the $a_{13} = \frac{1}{2}, a_{31} = 2$ to be the missing values, namely, the corresponding incomplete PCM is:

$$\begin{pmatrix} 1 & \frac{1}{9} & \times & \frac{1}{5} \\ 9 & 1 & 5 & 2 \\ \times & \frac{1}{5} & 1 & \frac{1}{2} \\ 5 & \frac{1}{2} & 2 & 1 \end{pmatrix}$$

Introduce the IBMM to estimate the missing values.

Step 1: Assume $a_{13} = x$, $a_{13} = \frac{1}{x}$ then the revised pairwise comparison matrix (PCM) A with unknown variables x becomes

$$\begin{pmatrix} 1 & \frac{1}{9} & x & \frac{1}{5} \\ 9 & 1 & 5 & 2 \\ \frac{1}{x} & \frac{1}{5} & 1 & \frac{1}{2} \\ 5 & \frac{1}{2} & 2 & 1 \end{pmatrix}$$

Step 2: The induced bias matrix $C = AA - nA$ is

$$\begin{pmatrix} 0 & -\frac{11}{90} + \frac{x}{5} & -2x + \frac{43}{45} & -\frac{8}{45} + \frac{x}{2} \\ -8 + \frac{5}{x} & 0 & 9x - 6 & \frac{3}{10} \\ -\frac{2}{x} + \frac{43}{10} & \frac{1}{9x} - \frac{3}{20} & 0 & \frac{1}{5x} - \frac{3}{5} \\ -\frac{11}{2} + \frac{2}{x} & -\frac{2}{45} & 5x - \frac{3}{2} & 0 \end{pmatrix}$$

Step 3: Minimize all bias entries of the induced bias matrix C, that is, let all entries with unknown variables be equal to zeros, and then the following equations hold: System of equations generated from the upper triangular entries: 1st Column, 2rd Column and 3th Column respectively.

$$\left\{ -\frac{11}{90} + \frac{x}{5} = 0 \right. \qquad \left\{ \begin{array}{l} -2x + \frac{43}{45} = 0 \\ 9x - 6 = 0 \end{array} \right. \qquad \left\{ \begin{array}{l} -\frac{8}{45} + \frac{x}{2} \\ \frac{1}{5x} - \frac{3}{5} \end{array} \right.$$

System of equations generated from the lower triangular entries: first Column, second Column and third Column respectively.

$$\left\{ \begin{array}{l} -8 + \frac{5}{x} = 0 \\ -\frac{2}{x} + \frac{43}{10} = 0 \\ -\frac{11}{2} + \frac{2}{x} = 0 \end{array} \right. \qquad \left\{ \frac{1}{9x} - \frac{3}{20} = 0 \right. \qquad \left\{ 5x - \frac{3}{2} = 0 \right.$$

Step 4: Solve one of the above two systems of equations, then the solutions of the equations can be found. To compare both solutions, here, two systems of equations are all solved and the corresponding solutions can be found as follows: The first solutions of the upper triangular equations are

$$\{x_1 = 0.6111 \qquad \left\{ \begin{array}{l} x_2 = 0.4778 \\ x_3 = 0.6667 \end{array} \right. \qquad \left\{ \begin{array}{l} x_4 = 0.3556 \\ x_5 = 0.3333 \end{array} \right.$$

where x_i denotes the corresponding solution of the equations in the upper triangular matrix.
The second solutions of the lower triangular equations are

$$\left\{ \begin{array}{l} x_{21} = 0.6250 \\ x_{31} = 0.4651 \\ x_{41} = 0.3636 \end{array} \right. \qquad \{x_{32} = 0.7407 \qquad \{x_{43} = 0.3000$$

where x_{ij} denotes the corresponding solution of the equations located in i^{th} row and j^{th} column of the lower triangular matrix in the induced matrix.
Step 5: Average all solutions in order to keep the global consistency and get the optimal of variables.

Average the first solutions, then

$$x = \frac{x_1 + x_2 + x_3 + x_4 + x_5}{5} = \frac{2.4445}{5} = 0.4889$$

Average the second solutions, then

$$x = \frac{x_{21} + x_{31} + x_{41} + x_{32} + x_{43}}{5} = \frac{2.4944}{5} = 0.4989$$

The two averaged values from upper and lower triangular matrix are approximately equal to each other. We can use one of the values as the optimal value to replace the missing entries. According to the rule of 9-point scales by Saaty (1977), select a value from the scales $\frac{1}{9}$ to 9, which is closest to the averaged solution, as the final optimal value for the missing value. The closest value in this example is 0.5, which is consistent with the original value 0.5.

Step 6: Replace the missing value with the optimal values and test its consistency to guarantee it passes the consistency test.

No matter use 0.4889, or 0.4989 or their average value, 0.4939, or its closest value in the 9-point scale, that is, 0.5, as the missing value, the revised RPCM passes the consistency test.

For instance, we use the average of both solutions, 0.4939, as the optimal value, then, the revised PCM is.

$$A = \begin{pmatrix} 1 & \frac{1}{9} & 0.4939 & \frac{1}{5} \\ 9 & 1 & 5 & 2 \\ \frac{1}{0.4939} & \frac{1}{5} & 1 & \frac{1}{2} \\ 5 & \frac{1}{2} & 2 & 1 \end{pmatrix}$$

Calculate the maximum eigenvalue, then we can get $\lambda_{max} = 4.00745$, the consistency ratio CR $= 0.00279$, which are extremely close to the original values, $\lambda_{max} = 4.0076$ and CR $= 0.00284$. Thus, the missing values in the pairwise comparison matrix can be estimated by the IBMM.

References

Ergu D, Kou G, Peng Y, Shi Y, Shi Yu (2011c) BIMM: a bias induced matrix model for incomplete reciprocal pairwise comparison matrix. J Multi-Crit Decis Anal. doi:10.1002/mcda.472

Saaty TL (1977) A scaling method for priorities in hierarchical structures. J Math Psychol 15(3):234–281

Chapter 5
IBMM for Questionnaire Design Improvement

Questionnaire survey is a commonly used way to collect opinions and views in AHP/ANP. However, many factors such as tedious design format, redundant content, long length etc, may lead to inconsistent comparison matrix for the decision problem. Invalid or bad results of a questionnaire survey may cause the decision makers to make wrong decision. Furthermore, in the AHP/ANP, the score items for a comparison matrix in a questionnaire increase drastically if there are more comparisons, which result in longer survey.

In the previous Chapter, the IBMM is proposed to estimate the missing values of the pairwise comparison matrix (PCM). In Ergu and Kou (2011), the IBMM for estimating the missing values was further applied to the improvement of questionnaire design. Specifically, a scale format is used to design the score items for a comparison matrix in questionnaire survey. Besides, the IBMM is used to estimate the missing item scores of the reciprocal pairwise comparison matrix. The survey questionnaire can be improved according to the importance of score items and emergency degree of the surveyed questions. Details are described in this Chapter.

5.1 Motivation of the Research

The unconventional emergency decision maker should identify the related influence factors and make the decision rapidly. However, the decision making process is complicated because of the uncertain and unconventional features of emergency and the limited expertise. For instance, experts in different regions can fill questionnaire through distributed information communication technology system and provide suggestions to the decision maker. A problem statement and objective must be developed for the questionnaire. In addition, the problem and objectives should be decomposed into a hierarchy where each level is composed of the related attributes

G. Kou et al., *Data Processing for the AHP/ANP*, Quantitative Management 1,
DOI 10.1007/978-3-642-29213-2_5, © Springer-Verlag Berlin Heidelberg 2013

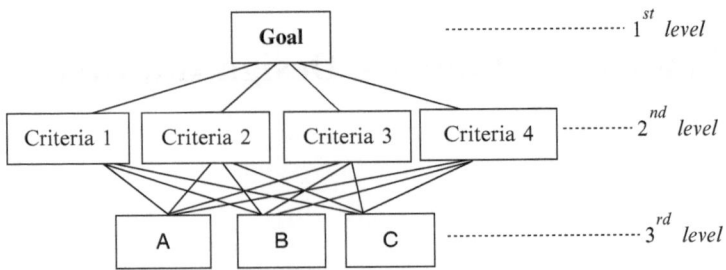

Fig. 5.1 The typical hierarchy structure with three levels in the AHP

or criteria when the AHP is used.[1] The score items should be designed for each PCM in order to collect the information and experts' views through questionnaire survey.

In the analytical hierarchy process (AHP), a complicated decision problem can be decomposed into several hierarchies according to the related attributes or criteria. The typical AHP hierarchy structure with three levels is shown in Fig. 5.1.

In the first level, there is a four-by-four comparison matrix with respect to the Goal, which contains 16 entries. In the second level, there are four three-by-three comparison matrices with respect to Criteria 1, Criteria 2, Criteria 3, Criteria 4, respectively. The total number of entries in the second level is 36. According to reciprocal rule, 18 score items are needed in a questionnaire. Likewise, for a typical 3-level hierarchy structure of AHP with m criteria and n alternatives, there is an m-by-m comparison matrix with respect to the Goal containing $m \times m$ entries in the first level, and there are m numbers of $n \times n$ comparison matrices totally containing mn^2 entries in the second level. According to the reciprocal property of one reciprocal PCM, there are only $n(n-1)/2$ comparisons to be compared for one $n \times n$ reciprocal PCM. The required comparisons in the first level are $m(m-1)/2$ while there are $m[n(n-1)/2]$ comparisons in the second level. Thus, the total number of required comparisons in this typical hierarchy structure is

$$m(m - 1)/2 + m[n (n - 1)/2] \tag{5.1}$$

Hence, there are $m(m-1)/2 + m[n(n-1)/2]$ involved score items. The item number will increase quickly with the increase of m and n, which directly result in longer survey, and may lead to comparison inconsistency or incomplete item scores. To resolve the both issues, the size of one comparison matrix in AHP (Millet and Harker 1990; Lim and Swenseth 1993), as well as the missing values estimation methods for incomplete reciprocal PCM (Fedrizzi and Giove 2007; Chiclana et al 2009), have been extensively studied.

---

[1] Since ANP is a generalization of the AHP, and AHP is the special case of ANP, therefore, the improvement of questionnaire design in AHP by IBMM is only addressed in this Chapter.

However, the number of attributes or criteria can not be reduced arbitrarily in order to reflect the nature of the decision problem, especially in the decision making process for unconventional emergency. The score items of a questionnaire survey designed for the comparison matrix can be reduced by deliberately ignoring some comparisons which are relatively unimportant or non-emergent. Then, the missing values can be estimated by using some missing value processing methods. Thus, the structure of questionnaire survey can be improved. In addition, the simplified structure can promote the respondents to fill in the questionnaire survey carefully, which can increase the response rate and guarantee a reliable surveyed result. Therefore, the motivation of this research includes the following three aspects.

1. Improve questionnaire design given m and n to reduce the length of a questionnaire
2. Assure the consistency of reciprocal PCM
3. Support rapid and efficient emergency decision making

The objective of this research is to improve questionnaire design and process the uncertain or missing item scores for rapid and efficient decision making using the IBMM method. The principles are presented below.

5.2   The Principles of Improving the Questionnaire Design

According to the importance and emergency of unconventional emergency, the emergency system should differentiate the information of unconventional emergency to provide differentiated services for unconventional emergencies in different ranks. Based on the theorem of the proposed IBMM for an incomplete PCM, we can deliberately ignore some comparisons according to the importance and emergency of the score items, which will reduce the number of score items and improve questionnaire survey design for rapid and efficient decision making. The missing values can be estimated using the IBMM technique once the questionnaire survey data are collected. To assist the decision makers to rapidly collect the related information in terms of the importance and emergency of score items, the general improving principle, the format of scale and three design formats are developed.

The General Improving Principle: Ignore some comparisons of the score items from 1 to $n(n-1)/4$ for each PCM in terms of the importance and relevance of the score items to improve the questionnaire design, where n is the size of the PCM. The missing comparisons can not be located at the same row or same column if the number of missing comparisons is $n(n-1)/4$, which is the maximum missing number estimated by IBMM.

Since the single PCM possesses the characteristics of all PCMs, the method for single PCM can be copied and applied to all other PCMs. In the following, a general PCM with four orders is used as an example to show the process of *The General Improving Principle*. According to the above principle, the following three cases with missing comparisons for such PCM can be set in terms of the importance and relevance of the score items. For an $n \times n$ PCM with p missing comparisons, there are $C_{n(n-1)/2}^{p}$ possible missing cases, where C denotes combination function.

$$
\begin{bmatrix}
1 & a_{12} & a_{13} & a_{14} \\
  & 1 & a_{23} & a_{24} \\
  &   & 1 & a_{34} \\
  &   &   & 1
\end{bmatrix}
\tag{5.2}
$$

1. Ignore one missing comparison

    In this case, there are six possible states for a PCM with four orders, as shown below.

$$
\begin{bmatrix}
1 & x & a_{13} & a_{14} \\
  & 1 & a_{23} & a_{24} \\
  &   & 1 & a_{34} \\
  &   &   & 1
\end{bmatrix}
\begin{bmatrix}
1 & a_{12} & x & a_{14} \\
  & 1 & a_{23} & a_{24} \\
  &   & 1 & a_{34} \\
  &   &   & 1
\end{bmatrix}
\begin{bmatrix}
1 & a_{12} & a_{13} & x \\
  & 1 & a_{23} & a_{24} \\
  &   & 1 & a_{34} \\
  &   &   & 1
\end{bmatrix}
$$

$$
\begin{bmatrix}
1 & a_{12} & a_{13} & a_{14} \\
  & 1 & x & a_{24} \\
  &   & 1 & a_{34} \\
  &   &   & 1
\end{bmatrix}
\begin{bmatrix}
1 & a_{12} & a_{13} & a_{14} \\
  & 1 & a_{23} & x \\
  &   & 1 & a_{34} \\
  &   &   & 1
\end{bmatrix}
\begin{bmatrix}
1 & a_{12} & a_{13} & a_{14} \\
  & 1 & a_{23} & a_{24} \\
  &   & 1 & x \\
  &   &   & 1
\end{bmatrix}
$$

2. Ignore two missing comparisons

    In this case, there are $C_6^2 = 15$ possible states, and four of them are shown below as examples.

$$
\begin{bmatrix}
1 & x & y & a_{14} \\
  & 1 & a_{23} & a_{24} \\
  &   & 1 & a_{34} \\
  &   &   & 1
\end{bmatrix},
\begin{bmatrix}
1 & x & a_{13} & y \\
  & 1 & a_{23} & a_{24} \\
  &   & 1 & a_{34} \\
  &   &   & 1
\end{bmatrix},
\begin{bmatrix}
1 & x & a_{13} & a_{14} \\
  & 1 & y & a_{24} \\
  &   & 1 & a_{34} \\
  &   &   & 1
\end{bmatrix},
\begin{bmatrix}
1 & x & a_{13} & a_{14} \\
  & 1 & a_{23} & y \\
  &   & 1 & a_{34} \\
  &   &   & 1
\end{bmatrix}
$$

3. Ignore three missing comparisons

    In this case, there are $C_6^3 = 20$ possible states. Four of them are shown below as instances.

$$
\begin{bmatrix}
1 & x & y & a_{14} \\
  & 1 & z & a_{24} \\
  &   & 1 & a_{34} \\
  &   &   & 1
\end{bmatrix},
\begin{bmatrix}
1 & x & y & a_{14} \\
  & 1 & a_{23} & z \\
  &   & 1 & a_{34} \\
  &   &   & 1
\end{bmatrix},
\begin{bmatrix}
1 & x & y & a_{14} \\
  & 1 & a_{23} & a_{24} \\
  &   & 1 & z \\
  &   &   & 1
\end{bmatrix},
\begin{bmatrix}
1 & x & a_{13} & y \\
  & 1 & z & a_{24} \\
  &   & 1 & a_{34} \\
  &   &   & 1
\end{bmatrix}
$$

According to the *General Improving Principle*, the following four cases should be avoided since all values in corresponding row or column are unknown\missing except the values located at the main diagonal.

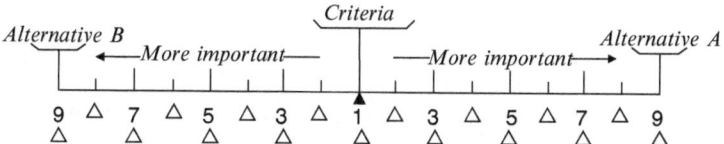

Note: *1 - Equal importance ; 3 -Weak importance ; 5 -Strong importance ;*
7 - Demonstrated importance; 9 - Absolute importance;
2,4,6,8 - Intermediate values between the two adjacent judgments
Tick " √   " the corresponding score in the symbol " △"

Fig. 5.2 The general format designed to compare two alternatives with respect to one criterion in a questionnaire survey design

$$
(a)\begin{bmatrix} 1 & \times & \times & \times \\ & 1 & a_{23} & a_{24} \\ & & 1 & a_{34} \\ & & & 1 \end{bmatrix} \quad (b)\begin{bmatrix} 1 & a_{12} & a_{13} & \times \\ & 1 & a_{23} & \times \\ & & 1 & \times \\ & & & 1 \end{bmatrix}
$$

$$
(c)\begin{bmatrix} 1 & a_{12} & \times & a_{14} \\ & 1 & \times & a_{23} \\ & & 1 & \times \\ & & & 1 \end{bmatrix} \quad (d)\begin{bmatrix} 1 & \times & a_{13} & a_{14} \\ & 1 & \times & \times \\ & & 1 & a_{34} \\ & & & 1 \end{bmatrix}
$$

To the maximum missing comparisons estimated by the IBMM, the number of comparisons mentioned in equation (5.1) can be reduced to $\{m(m-1)/2 + m[n(n-1)/2]\}/2$. Besides, any of the above missing formats can reduce the number of comparison, and the missing value can be estimated by the IBMM method while the consistency is kept. For instance, assume that we need to design score items in a questionnaire survey for selecting the best emergency alternatives among three provided alternatives with respect to the attribute. We can design the score items for the corresponding comparison matrix in the questionnaire survey as follows, and take two of them to the questionnaire survey. This example will be illustrated after the method of the *Format of Scale* is introduced.

The Format of Scale: In order to present the relationship between two alternatives with respect to one criterion, the following two formats as shown in Figs. 5.2 and 5.3, the scale combined with 9-point scale proposed by Saaty (2001), is proposed to score the items for the respondents.

Figure 5.2 is the normal format used to compare two alternatives with respect to one criterion in a questionnaire survey design. In Fig. 5.3, the score "0" is added to this scale denoting the uncertain item in order to reflect the real judgment situation.

According to the above design format, the design for selecting the emergence alternatives mentioned above can be designed as shown in Fig.5.4.

Based on the above general improving principle and the format of scale, the following three types of formats are proposed to design a questionnaire survey for a PCM in terms of the importance of score items and corresponding emergency degree in order to provide differentiated services for unconventional emergency in different ranks.

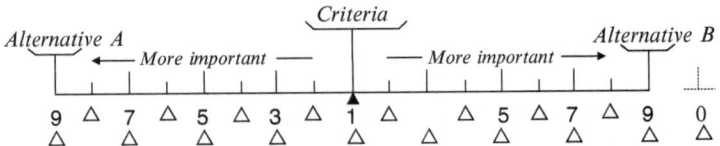

Note: *1 – Equal importance; 3 – Weak importance; 5 – Strong importance;*
7 – Demonstrated importance; 9 – Absolute importance;
2,4,6,7 – Intermediate values between the two adjacent judgments
0 - Uncertain
Tick "√" the corresponding score in the symbol "△"

Fig. 5.3 The general format with uncertainty designed to compare two alternatives with respect to one criteria in a questionnaire survey design

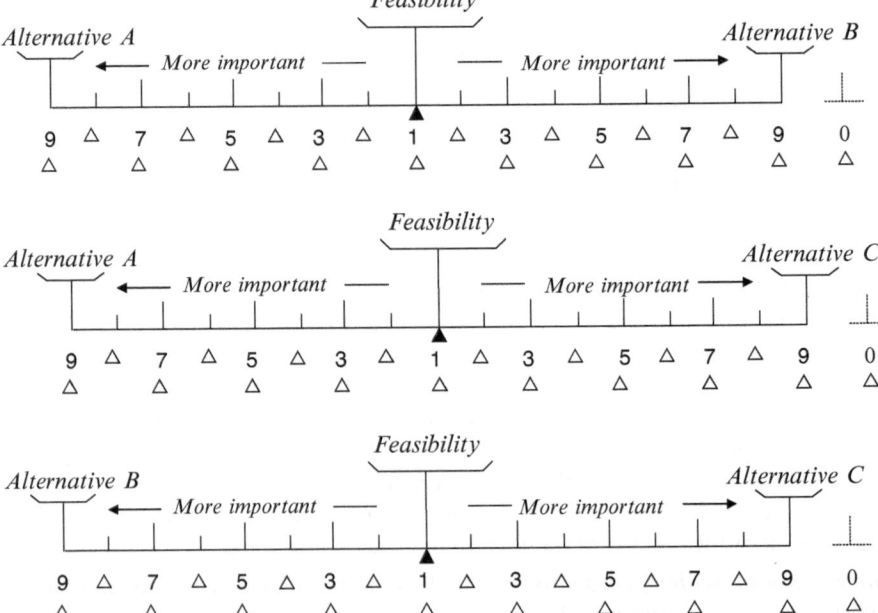

Fig. 5.4 The questionnaire design using general format with uncertainty for selecting the emergence alternatives with respect to feasibility

Design Format 1: Use the formal format without the uncertain factor to design a questionnaire survey.

Design Format 2: Use the general format with uncertain factor as shown in Fig. 5.2 to design a questionnaire survey.

Design Format 3: Skip some score items in terms of above principals to design a questionnaire survey.

Table 5.1 The general PCM with four orders

Goal	C1	C2	C3	C4
C1	1	a_{12}	a_{13}	a_{14}
C2		1	a_{23}	a_{24}
C3			1	a_{34}
C4				1

The first type of design format is a commonly used format. For the second type of design format, the uncertain score factor (item) is added to the scale score item comparing the first one, which is a common situation during filling a questionnaire survey because of the respondents' limited expertise and/or preference conflicts. Although the set of uncertain item may cause some irresponsible respondents to select more than the maximum number of missing comparison estimated by IBMM, and lead to the invalid response, it is still better than arbitrary selection which may result in the wrong decision making. For the third type of design format, the missing number of comparison can be set from 1 to $n(n-1)/4$ to reduce the number of score items. This type of design format is designed for rapid and efficient decision making, especially for unconventional emergency decision making. When we choose the maximum missing comparisons in a questionnaire design, the missing comparisons or the corresponding reciprocal missing comparisons should not be located at the same row or same column.

In order to demonstrate the above design formats, the following PCM with four orders as shown in Table 5.1 is used as an example.

When score items are designed for this comparison matrix in a questionnaire survey, the second type of design format can be used, for instance, the design of score items for the PCM is as shown in Fig. 5.5.

In an unconventional emergency scenario, the above design format can further be improved by ignoring some comparisons. For instance, ignoring three comparisons using the *design format 3* as shown in Fig. 5.6.

Comparing with previous two design formats, the third design format will increase double information gathering speed if the maximum missing method is used, which is very important for rapid and efficient unconventional emergency decision making.

5.3 Illustrative Example

In order to show the process of improving a questionnaire design using the second and third types of design format and estimating the missing score items, an example about H1N1 flu is introduced in this section. Since the processes of designing a score item and estimating a missing score item for single comparison matrix can be copied and applied to all others comparison matrices, in this section, we only focus on single comparison matrix with four orders.

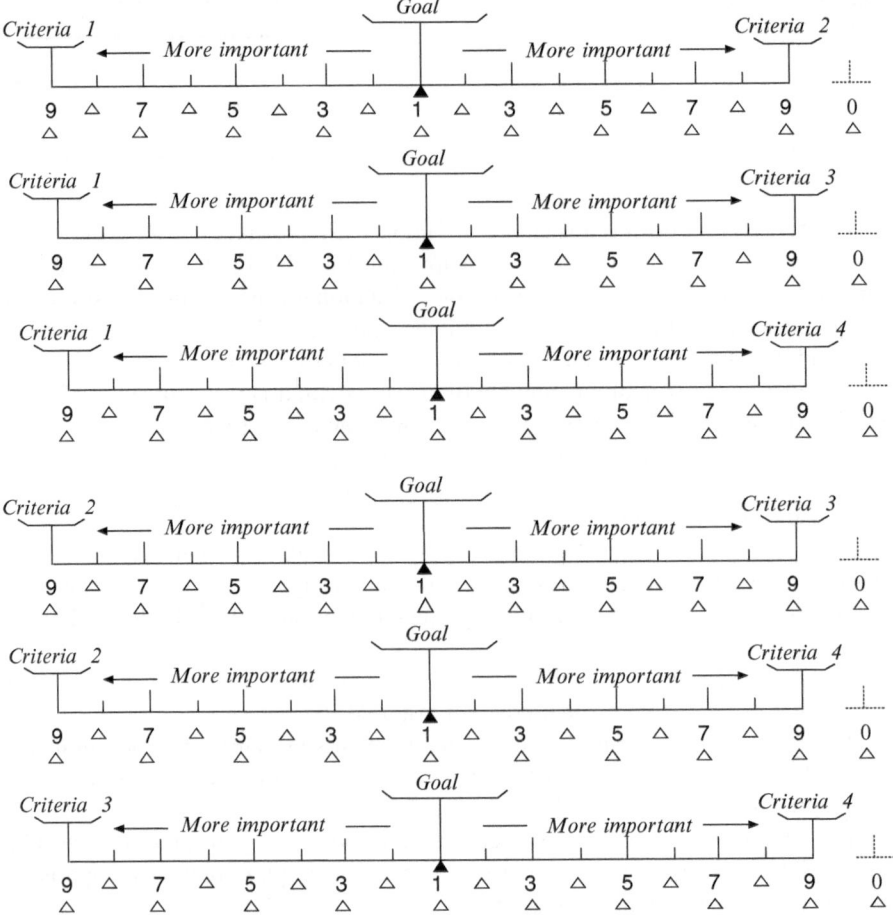

Fig. 5.5 The design format of score items with uncertain factor for a PCM with four orders

In year 2009, the outbreak of H1N1 flu had caused a huge panic. At the beginning, it was difficult to identify whether it was H1N1 flu or just a seasonal flu since the symptoms of H1N1 were similar to seasonal flu. In such scenario, assume a hospital located at remote region received a patient who just came back by plane from Mexico accompanying the following symptoms such as Fever, Runny, Confusion and Vomiting. The doctors could not make decision whether it was H1N1 flu or a seasonal flu because of the limited expertise about H1N1. Therefore, they decided to advise some related experts through the telemedicine systems of this hospital and make decision using the AHP embedded in the telemedicine systems. Assume the advice can normally be done through questionnaire conveyed by telemedicine systems. According to the design format 2 and format 3, we can classify the questionnaire design into two steps. First, design a short questionnaire

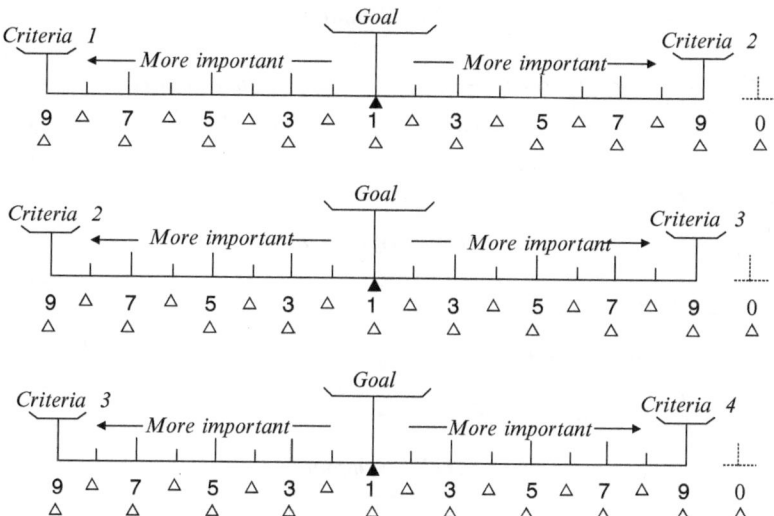

Fig. 5.6 The design format for a PCM with four orders by ignoring three comparisons

Table 5.2 The 4×4 PCM for H1N1 symptoms

H1N1 symptoms	Fever	Runny	Confusion	Vomiting
Fever	1	a_{12}	a_{13}	a_{14}
Runny		1	a_{23}	a_{24}
Confusion			1	a_{34}
Vomiting				1

using the design format 3 for this unconventional emergency in order to collect the data from experts rapidly. Second, design a questionnaire using design format 1 and design format 2 to validate the results obtained from first questionnaire. The three kinds of design formats can also be used simultaneously.

In order to validate the results of design format 2 and 3 using the results of design format 1, the design format 1 is introduced as case 1, design format 2 is presented as case 2, and the design format 3 is demonstrated as case 3. According to the patient's clinical symptoms, a 4×4 PCM for attributes Fever, Runny, Confusion and Vomiting with respect to H1N1 symptoms can be generated, as shown in Table 5.2. The following three cases are used to design and improve a questionnaire design for PCM.

Case 1 – Use the *Design Format 1* to design score items for this PCM, and assume that the following response is collected in one completed questionnaire.

Replace the corresponding entries with the data obtained from Fig. 5.7, and the PCM as shown in Table 5.3 is obtained. Calculate the maximum eigenvalue, consistency ratio (CR) and priority weights of this PCM, we can get $\lambda_{\max} = 4.0816$ and $CR = 0.0306$. The priority weights are shown in Table 5.3.

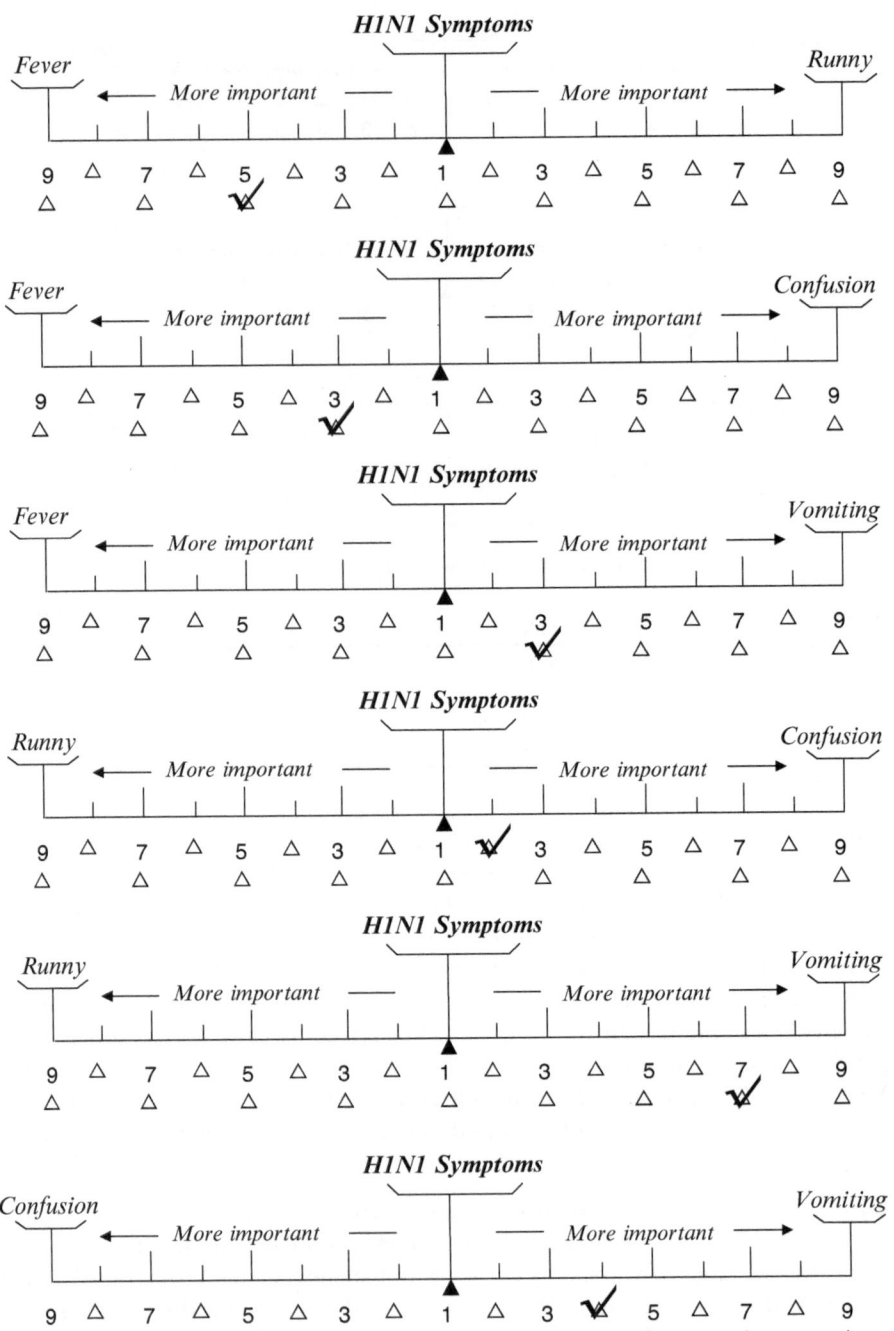

Fig. 5.7 The completed questionnaire designed by *Design Format 1*

Table 5.3 Single PCM with four orders obtained from questionnaire survey

H1N1 symptoms	Fever	Runny	Confusion	Vomiting	Priority weights
Fever	1	5	3	$\frac{1}{3}$	0.2713
Runny	$\frac{1}{5}$	1	$\frac{1}{2}$	$\frac{1}{7}$	0.0618
Confusion	$\frac{1}{3}$	2	1	$\frac{1}{4}$	0.1143
Vomiting	3	7	4	1	0.5527

Case 2 – Design the score items for this PCM in a questionnaire by using *Design Format 2*. Assume one of the completed questionnaires is listed in Fig. 5.8.

From this questionnaire, the following incomplete PCM with two missing comparisons, as shown in Table 5.4, can be obtained.

Apply the IBMM method to this incomplete comparison matrix and estimate the two missing comparisons. The brief estimation steps are as follows:

Step 1: Replace the two missing values with unknown variables $x, 1/x; y, 1/y$ as shown below

$$\begin{pmatrix} 1 & x & 3 & \frac{1}{3} \\ \frac{1}{x} & 1 & y & \frac{1}{7} \\ \frac{1}{3} & \frac{1}{y} & 1 & \frac{1}{4} \\ 3 & 7 & 4 & 1 \end{pmatrix}$$

Step 2: Calculate the induced bias matrix C using the IBMM formula $C = AA - nA$.

Step 3: Set all entries with unknown variables be zeros in the upper triangular matrix, and get six number of equations.

Step 4: Solve pairwise combined systems of linear equations.

Step 5: Average all solutions and find the optimal values of variables. The results of calculation are $x = 2.86$ and $y = 0.5850$. Therefore, the corresponding values located at the 9-point scale are 3 and 1/2 respectively.

Step 6: Replace the unknown variables with 3 and 1/2, then calculate the maximum eigenvalue, CR, and priority weights for the revised PCM, we get

$$\lambda_{\max} = 4.0206, \quad CR = 0.0077, \quad W = (\,0.2240 \quad 0.0737 \quad 0.1330 \quad 0.5693\,)$$

Likewise, we can deliberately ignore any two of comparisons in above PCM (as shown in Table 5.2), then estimate them using the IBMM. The results are shown in Table 5.5.

Case 3 – Since the decision making for this emergent event needs to be made as soon as possible, we design the score items for a questionnaire using *Design Format 3*, and assume one of the questionnaires was filled as Fig. 5.9.

Transform the corresponding scale scores to the following incomplete PCM, which is shown in Table 5.6.

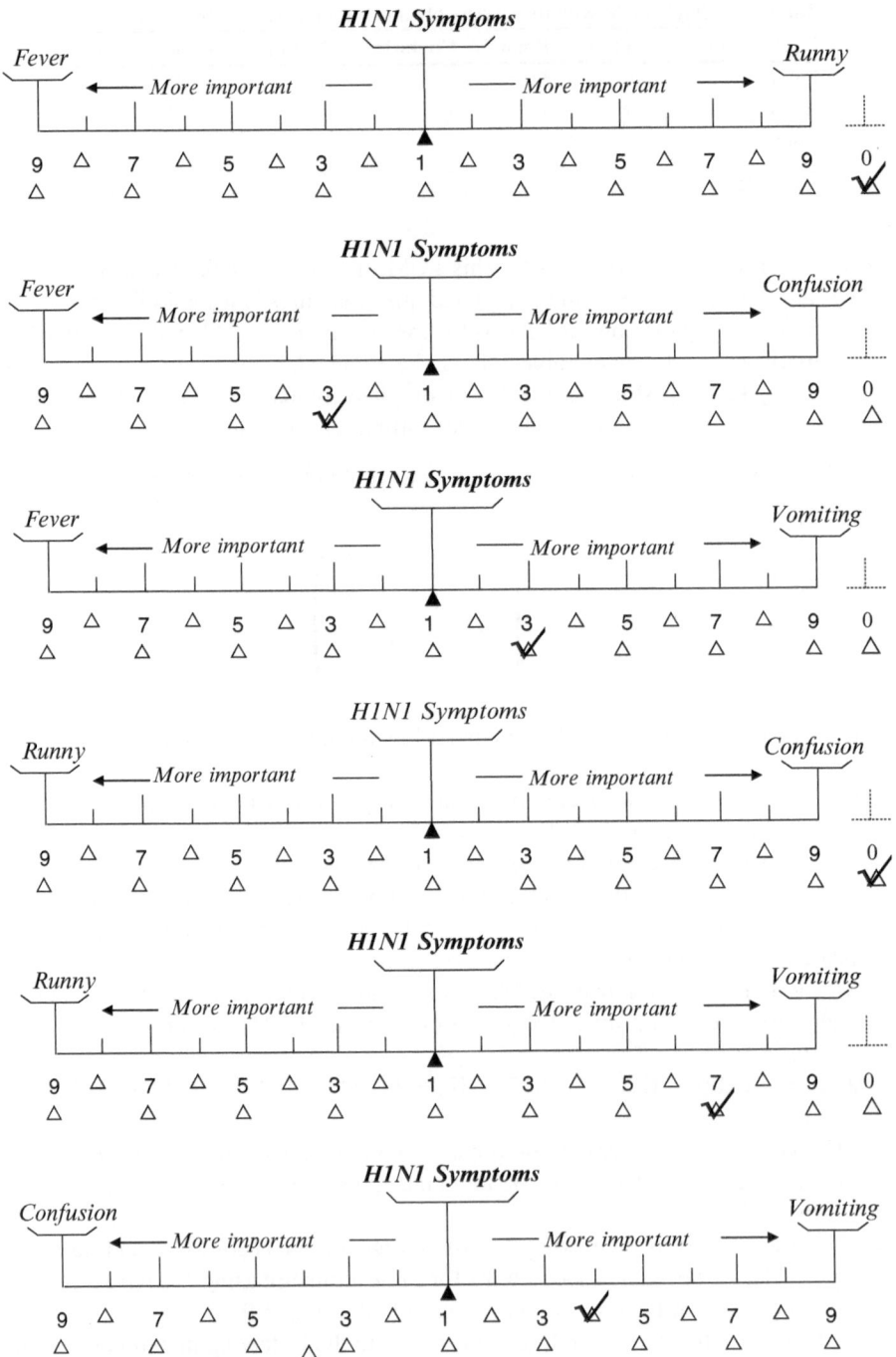

Fig. 5.8 The completed questionnaire designed by *Design Format 2*

Table 5.4 Single incomplete PCM with four orders obtained from above questionnaire survey

H1N1 symptoms	Fever	Runny	Confusion	Vomiting
Fever	1	×	3	$\frac{1}{3}$
Runny	×	1	×	$\frac{1}{7}$
Confusion	$\frac{1}{3}$	×	1	$\frac{1}{4}$
Vomiting	3	7	4	1

Table 5.5 The missing comparisons and corresponding estimated values in a 4 × 4 PCM

MC	EV	CV	OV	MC	EV	CV	OV
a_{12}	2.5322	3	5	a_{13}	2.4001	2 or 3	3
a_{13}	1.3123	2	3	a_{34}	0.2925	1/4	1/4
a_{12}	5.8920	6	5	a_{14}	0.7321	1/2	1/3
a_{14}	0.7970	1/2 or 1	1/3	a_{23}	0.5859	1/2	1/2
a_{12}	5.3003	5	5	a_{14}	0.7206	1/2	1/3
a_{23}	0.7633	1/2	1/2	a_{24}	0.1384	1/7	1/7
a_{12}	6.1746	6	5	a_{14}	0.7838	1/2	1/3
a_{24}	0.1197	1/7	1/7	a_{34}	0.2826	1/4	1/4
a_{12}	4.8677	5	5	a_{23}	0.6175	1/2	1/2
a_{34}	0.2318	1/4	1/4	a_{24}	0.1514	1/6	1/7
a_{13}	2.6644	3	3	a_{23}	0.7832	1/2	1/2
a_{14}	0.6902	1/2	1/3	a_{34}	0.2383	1/4	1/4
a_{13}	2.0444	2	3	a_{24}	0.0663	1/9	1/7
a_{24}	0.1021	1/7	1/7	a_{34}	0.1273	1/8	1/4

MC missing comparisons, *EV* estimated values, *CV* closest value within 9-point scale, *OV* original values

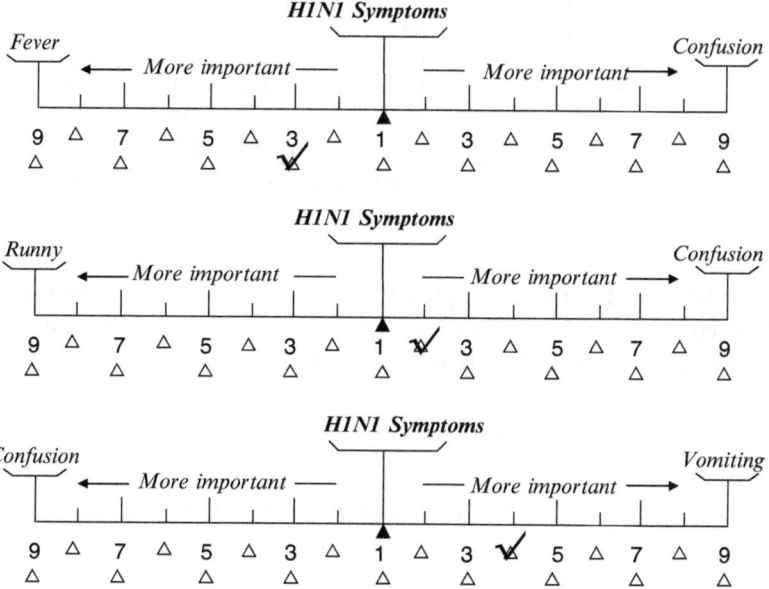

Fig. 5.9 The completed questionnaire designed by *Design Format 3*

Table 5.6 The incomplete
4×4 PCM with three missing
comparisons obtained from
above questionnaire survey

H1N1 symptoms	Fever	Runny	Confusion	Vomiting
Fever	1	×	3	×
Runny	×	1	$\frac{1}{2}$	×
Confusion	$\frac{1}{3}$	2	1	$\frac{1}{4}$
Vomiting	×	×	4	1

Table 5.7 The possible three missing comparisons, the corresponding estimated values, and the closest values located at 9-point scale

MC	EV	CV	OV	MC	EV	CV	OV
a_{12}	2.3333	3	5	a_{13}	2.8571	3	3
a_{13}	1.3333	2	3	a_{14}	0.7143	1/2	1/3
a_{23}	0.5714	1/2	1/2	a_{23}	0.5714	1/2	1/2
a_{12}	2.6667	3	5	a_{13}	2.5000	3	3
a_{13}	1.3333	2	3	a_{14}	0.6250	1/2	1/3
a_{24}	0.1250	1/7	1/7	a_{24}	0.1250	1/7	1/7
a_{12}	2.3333	3	5	a_{13}	2.5000	3	3
a_{13}	1.1667	1	3	a_{14}	0.7143	1	1/3
a_{34}	0.2857	1/4	1/4	a_{34}	0.2857	1/4	1/4
a_{12}	5.2500	5	5	a_{13}	1.3333	1 or 2	3
a_{14}	0.7500	1 or 1/2	1/3	a_{23}	0.2667	1/2	1/2
a_{23}	0.5714	1/2	1/2	a_{24}	0.0667	1/9	1/7
a_{12}	6.0000	6	5	a_{13}	2.5000	3	3
a_{14}	0.7500	1 or 1/2	1/3	a_{24}	0.0667	1/9	1/7
a_{24}	0.1250	1/7	1/7	a_{34}	0.1333	1/7	1/4
a_{12}	6.0000	6	5	a_{14}	0.7500	1 or 1/2	1/3
a_{14}	0.8571	1 or 1/2	1/3	a_{23}	0.6000	1/2	1/2
a_{34}	0.2857	1/4	1/4	a_{24}	0.1500	1/7	1/7
a_{12}	2.3333	2 or 3	5	a_{14}	0.7143	1 or 1/2	1/3
a_{23}	1.2857	1 or 2	1/2	a_{23}	0.6000	1/2	1/2
a_{34}	0.1111	1/7	1/4	a_{34}	0.2381	1/4	1/4
a_{12}	6.0000	6	5	a_{23}	0.6000	1/2	1/2
a_{24}	0.0556	1/9	1/7	a_{24}	0.0667	1/9	1/7
a_{34}	0.1111	1/7	1/4	a_{34}	0.1111	1/7	1/4

MC missing comparisons, *EV* estimated values, *CV* closest value within 9-point scale, *OV* original values

Apply the IBMM to this incomplete PCM and estimate the missing values. The estimated missing values, maximum eigenvalue of the revised PCM, the CR, and the corresponding priority weights are shown below:

$$a_{12} = 6, a_{14} = 0.75, \text{ and } a_{24} = 0.125; \lambda_{\max} = 4.0297, CR = 0.0111,$$

$$W = (\ 0.3186 \quad 0.0605 \quad 0.1166 \quad 0.5042\ )$$

Table 5.8 The comparisons of the results obtained from three cases

	λ_{max}	CR	Priority weights			
			Fever	Runny	Confusion	Vomiting
Case 1	4.0816	0.0306	0.2713	0.0618	0.1143	0.5527
Case 2	4.0206	0.0077	0.2240	0.0737	0.1330	0.5693
Case 3	4.0297	0.0111	0.3186	0.0605	0.1166	0.5042

Similarly, there are 16 different kinds of incomplete PCM with three missing comparisons. The questionnaire can be designed into 16 different formats in terms of the importance and emergency of the score items. The possible kinds of three missing comparisons, the corresponding estimated values, and the closest values located at 9-point scale are shown in Table 5.7.

According to the results obtained from above three cases, the comparisons among the λ_{max}, CR, and the corresponding priority weights are shown in Table 5.8.

It can be seen from Table 5.8 that the maximum eigenvalues and the CRs of both revised PCM are smaller than that of the complete PCM, however, the ranks of priority vectors are the same, that is, compared with the seasonal flu, the ranks of the symptoms of H1N1 flu are Vomiting, Fever, Confusion and Runny. The results of comparisons show that the questionnaire can be designed using *Design Format 2* and *Design Format 3*. The score items are reduced and the questionnaire is improved, which is extremely important for rapid and efficient unconventional emergency decision making.

References

Chiclana F, Herrera-Viedma E, Alonso S (2009) A note on two methods for estimating missing pairwise preference values. IEEE Trans Syst Man Cybernet B Cybernet 39:1628–1633

Ergu D, Kou G (2011) Questionnaire design improvement and missing item scores estimation for rapid and efficient decision making. Ann Oper Res 2011. doi:10.1007/s10479-011-0922-3

Fedrizzi M, Giove S (2007) Incomplete pairwise comparison and consistency optimization. Eur J Oper Res, Elsevier, 183(1):303–313

Lim KH, Swenseth SR (1993) An iterative procedure for reducing problem size in large scale AHP problems. Eur J Oper Res 67:64–74

Millet I, Harker PT (1990) Globally effective questioning in the analytic hierarchy process. Eur J Oper Res 48:88–97

Saaty TL (2001) Deriving the AHP 1–9 scale from first principles. In: ISAHP 2001 proceedings, Bern, Switzerland

Chapter 6
IBMM for Rank Reversal

When a new alternative or criterion is added to the decision model or old ones are deleted from the decision matrix, the rank of the alternatives may be reversed, namely, a less preferred alternative may become more preferred. In this Chapter, the IBMM is further extended to perform the sensitivity analysis of rank reversal when a new alternative or criterion is added or old ones are deleted. Details are described below.

6.1 Rank Reversal Issue in the AHP/ANP

Since Belton and Gear (1983) proposed the rank reversal problem by an example in AHP, the rank reversal problem has been extensively studied (Saaty and Vargas 1993; Millet and Saaty 2000; Triantaphyllou 2004; Wijnmalen and Wedley 2008). There are two situations which may cause rank reversal, that is, adding new alternatives/criteria or deleting old ones. Rank reversal is attributed to the use of relative measurement and normalization (Saaty 2001b).

However, there are few data processing models which can analyze the sensitivity or identify the critical values of rank reversal. In the process of decision making, lots of criteria should be taken into consideration in order to make the valid decision making. If new alternative or criterion is added in the decision process, the rank of alternatives may be reversed, and a less preferred alternative may become more preferred. In Ergu et al. (2011g), the IBMM is creatively applied to explore and analyze the sensitivity of rank reversal and is introduced as the procedure to determine the critical values of rank reversal. Without losing generality, in the remaining part of this Chapter, we will only discuss the case that a new criterion or an alternative is added. The specific processes of sensitivity analysis of rank reversal will be briefly presented next.

6.2   Sensitivity Analysis of Rank Reversal by the IBMM

In this section, the IBMM is further introduced to determine the reversal points of rank reversal. The steps for sensitivity analysis of rank reversal are as follows.

1. When a criterion or alternative is added, append a new row and a corresponding column with unknown variables denoted as x, y, z, etc. to the existing PCM.
2. Apply the IBMM to create a system of relation equations for the unknown variables.
3. Solve the equations by combining the 9-point scale as a constraint to estimate the range of the unknown variables.
4. Estimate the reversal points of rank reversal by fixing one variable at a time in the sensitivity analysis.

6.3   Illustrative Examples

To analyze the sensitivity of rank reversal and identify the critical values of rank reversal by IBMM, assume a new alternative (in short, S4) is added to the following matrix S as shown in Table 6.1. The priority vectors of alternatives S1, S2 and S3 with respect to the criterion S are calculated and shown in Table 6.1. We compute below the priority vector of alternatives with respect to criterion S and found $S2 > S1 > S3$.

Assume a potential alternative, S4, is added. To determine the reversal points of rank reversal, and develop insights into the intrinsic relationship between alternatives, we follow the steps below.

Step 1: Add an alternative by creating a new row and column to matrix S using variables x, y, z and their reciprocals. The new matrix is denoted as S':

$$S' = \begin{pmatrix} 1 & 1/7 & 1 & x \\ 7 & 1 & 9 & y \\ 1 & 1/9 & 1 & z \\ 1/x & 1/y & 1/z & 1 \end{pmatrix}$$

Step 2: Apply the IBMM to this matrix. The induced bias matrix becomes

Table 6.1 The comparison matrix C and priority vectors of three alternatives

S	S1	S2	S3	Priority vector
S1	1	1/7	1	0.1049
S2	7	1	9	0.7986
S3	1	1/9	1	0.0965

$$C = \begin{pmatrix} 0 & -11/63 + x/y & -5/7 + x/z & -2x + y/7 + z \\ & 0 & -11 + y/z & 7x - 2y + 9z \\ & & 0 & x + y/9 - 2z \\ & & & 0 \end{pmatrix}$$

Step 3: Construct the constraint system of equations using the upper matrix.

$$\begin{cases} -11/63 + x/y = 0 \\ -5/7 + x/z = 0 \\ -11 + y/z = 0 \end{cases} \tag{6.1}$$

$$s.t. \begin{cases} 1/9 \le x \le 9 \\ 1/9 \le y \le 9 \\ 1/9 \le z \le 9 \end{cases}$$

$$\begin{cases} -2x + y/7 + z = 0 \\ 7x - 2y + 9z = 0 \\ x + y/9 - 2z = 0 \end{cases} \tag{6.2}$$

$$s.t. \begin{cases} 1/9 \le x \le 9 \\ 1/9 \le y \le 9 \\ 1/9 \le z \le 9 \end{cases}$$

Step 4: Solve the constrained systems of Eqs. (6.1) and (6.2). From (6.1), the relationships between x and y, x and z, and y and z can be determined, which are shown in Eq. (6.3). The relationships between any two of the variables can be further derived from Eqs. (6.2)–(6.3), e.g. the relationship between y and z is shown in Eq. (6.4).

$$\begin{cases} x = \dfrac{11}{63}y \\ x = \dfrac{5}{7}z \\ y = 11z \end{cases} \tag{6.3}$$

$$\begin{cases} y = \dfrac{45}{11}z \approx 4z \\[2mm] y = 11z \\[2mm] y = \dfrac{25}{3}z \approx 8z \\[2mm] y = \dfrac{189}{23}z \approx 8z \\[2mm] y = \dfrac{207}{25}z \approx 8z \end{cases} \tag{6.4}$$

To avoid estimating the missing data arbitrarily, the decision maker will focus on one pair of relationship first, say between y and z and answer: how much more important is y to z with respect to the criterion S? Suppose the decision maker chooses one of the closest relations that best describes his sentiment from Eq. (6.4), say y = 11z. We then apply it to Eq. (6.2) to further determine the relationship between x and z. Equation (6.2) thus becomes

$$\begin{cases} y = 11z \\[2mm] x = \dfrac{13}{7}z \\[2mm] x = \dfrac{7}{9}z \\[2mm] x = \dfrac{9}{7}z \end{cases} \tag{6.5}$$

Abiding by the constraint that $1/9 \le x, y, z \le 9$, in (6.5), we obtain

$$\begin{cases} 0.0101 \le z \le 0.8182 \\[1mm] 0.0598 \le z \le 4.4846 \\[1mm] 0.1429 \le z \le 11.5714 \\[1mm] 0.0864 \le z \le 7 \end{cases} \tag{6.6}$$

The ranges in (6.6) are reduced to $0.1429 \le Z \le 0.8182$, which is close to the interval $1/7 < z < 1$ in the 9-point integer scale used in AHP/ANP.

Step 5: Analyze the sensitivity of rank reversal. By applying the real constraint for z (i.e. $1/7 < z < 1$) to Eqs. (6.5) and (6.6), we can determine the ranges for x and y (see the middle parts of Tables 6.2, 6.3, 6.4, 6.5, 6.6, 6.7, and 6.8). Table 6.2 shows the sensitivity analysis of rank reversal when S4 is added and z = 1/5. Tables 6.3, 6.4, 6.5, 6.6, 6.7, and 6.8 below show the sensitivity analysis of rank reversal when the value of variable z varies at different level.

Table 6.2 Sensitivity analysis of rank reversal when variable $z = 1/5$

	$Y = 45z/11$	$Y = 25z/3$	$Y = 11z$
$z = 1/5$	0.8182	1.6667	2.2000
			$1 \leq Y \leq 2$
			$1/7 \leq X \leq 1/3$
X1 = 11y/63	0.1429	0.2910	0.3841
X2 = 5z/7	0.1429	0.1429	0.1429
X3 = (2y−9z)/7	−0.0234	0.2191	0.3714
X4 = 2z−y/9	0.3091	0.2148	0.1556
X5 = (y/7 + z)/2	0.1584	0.2191	0.2571

	$Y = 1$	$Y = 1$	$Y = 1$	$Y = 2$	$Y = 2$	$Y = 2$
	$X = 1/7$	$X = 1/5$	$X = 1/3$	$X = 1/7$	$X = 1/5$	$X = 1/3$
	Vectors	Vectors	Vectors	Vectors	Vectors	Vectors
S1	**0.0624**	0.0696	0.0828	**0.0615**	0.0683	0.0801
S2	0.4686	0.4822	0.4984	0.5437	0.5563	0.5703
S3	**0.0644**	0.0658	0.0675	**0.0620**	0.0639	0.0662
S4	0.4047	0.3823	0.3512	0.3328	0.3116	0.2834

Note: The rank reversal of S1 and S3 occurred in two places where two groups of the boundary values of variables are used. That is, x = 1/7 and y = 1; and x = 1/7 and y = 2

Table 6.3 The sensitivity analysis of rank reversal when the values of variable z is fixed (z = 1/7)

Z = 1/7	Y = 45z/11	Y = 25z/3	Y = 11z	
	0.5884	1.1905	1.5714	1/2 ≤ Y ≤ 2 1/9 ≤ X ≤ 1/4
X1 = 11y/63	0.1020	0.2079	0.2744	
X2 = 5z/7	0.1020	0.1020	0.1020	
X3 = (2y−9z)/7	−0.0167	0.1565	0.2653	
X4 = 2z−y/9	0.2208	0.1534	0.1111	
X5 = (y/7 + z)/2	0.1132	0.1507	0.1837	

	Y = 1/2 X = 1/9	Y = 1/2 X = 1/8	Y = 1/2 X = 1/4	Y = 1 X = 1/9	Y = 1 X = 1/8	Y = 1 X = 1/4	Y = 2 X = 1/9	Y = 2 X = 1/8	Y = 2 X = 1/4
	Priority	Priority	Priority	Priority	Priority	Priority	Priority	Priority	Priority
S1	**0.0539**	0.0562	0.0731	0.0559	0.0582	0.0740	0.0551	0.0572	0.0715
S2	0.3686	0.3735	0.3988	0.4441	0.4494	0.4753	0.5225	0.5274	0.5497
S3	**0.0551**	0.0556	0.0580	0.0559	0.0566	0.0599	0.0539	0.0547	0.0587
S4	0.5225	0.5147	0.4702	0.4441	0.4357	0.3908	0.3686	0.3607	0.3201

Note: The rank of S1 and S3 is reversed when the left boundary values of variables x, y, and z, are used. That is, x = 1/9, y = 1/2, and z = 1/7

Table 6.4 The sensitivity analysis of rank reversal when the values of variable z is fixed (z = 1/6)

z = 1/6	Y = 45z/11	Y = 25z/3	Y = 11z
	0.6818	1.3889	1.8333
		1/2 ≤ Y ≤ 2	1/8 ≤ X ≤ 1/4
X1 = 11y/63	0.1190	0.2425	0.3201
X2 = 5z/7	0.1190	0.1190	0.1190
X3 = (2y−9z)/7	−0.0195	0.1825	0.3095
X4 = 2z−y/9	0.2576	0.1790	0.1296
X5 = (y/7 + z)/2	0.1320	0.1825	0.2143

	Y = 1/2, X = 1/8	Y = 1/2, X = 1/7	Y = 1/2, X = 1/4	Y = 1, X = 1/8	Y = 1, X = 1/7	Y = 1, X = 1/4	Y = 2, X = 1/8	Y = 2, X = 1/7	Y = 2, X = 1/4
	Priority	Priority	Priority	Priority	Priority	Priority	Priority	Priority	Priority
S1	**0.0567**	0.0595	0.0733	**0.0589**	0.0616	0.0745	0.0581	0.0606	0.0723
S2	0.3798	0.3852	0.4051	0.4556	0.4615	0.4823	0.5325	0.5379	0.5561
S3	**0.0589**	0.0594	0.0611	**0.0598**	0.0605	0.0629	0.0575	0.0584	0.0615
S4	0.5045	0.4958	0.4605	0.4257	0.4164	0.3803	0.3519	0.3431	0.3100

Note: The rank reversal of S1 and S3 occurred in two places where two groups of the left boundary values of variables are used, and one group of the left boundary values is used. That is, x = 1/8 and y = 1/2; x = 1/8 and y = 1

Table 6.5 The sensitivity analysis of rank reversal when the values of variable z is fixed (z = 1/4)

z = 1/4	Y = 45z/11	Y = 25z/3	Y = 11z	Y = 1	Y = 1	Y = 1	Y = 2	Y = 2	Y = 2	Y = 3	Y = 3	Y = 3
	1.0227	2.0833	2.7500	X = 1/5	X = 1/4	X = 1/3	X = 1/4	X = 1/5	X = 1/3	X = 1/5	X = 1/4	X = 1/3
	1 ≤ Y ≤ 3	1/5 ≤ X ≤ 1/3		Priority	Priority	Priority	Priority	Priority	Priority	Priority	Priority	Priority
X1 = 11y/63	0.1786	0.3638	0.4802									
X2 = 5z/7	0.1786	0.1786	0.1786									
X3 = (2y−9z)/7	−0.0292	0.2738	0.4643									
X4 = 2z−y/9	0.3864	0.2685	0.1944									
X5 = (y/7 + z)/2	0.1981	0.2738	0.3214									
S1				**0.0703**	0.0755	0.0831	0.0755	0.074	0.0808	0.0692	0.0716	0.0779
S2				0.4905	0.4983	0.507	0.4983	0.5706	0.5783	0.5633	0.6116	0.6181
S3				**0.0710**	0.0716	0.0723	0.0716	0.0695	0.0706	0.0685	0.0667	0.0681
S4				0.3683	0.3545	0.3376	0.3545	0.2859	0.2703	0.2990	0.2501	0.2359

Note: The rank reversal of S1 and S3 only occurred when the left boundary values of variables are used, that is, $x = 1/5$ and $y = 1$.

Table 6.6 The sensitivity analysis of rank reversal when the values of variable z is fixed (z = 1/3)

z = 1/3	Y = 45z/11	Y = 25z/3	Y = 11z	1 ≤ Y ≤ 4	1/4 ≤ X ≤ 1/2	Y = 1	Y = 1	Y = 1	Y = 2	Y = 2	Y = 2	Y = 3	Y = 3	Y = 3
	1.3636	2.7778	3.6667			X = 1/4	X = 1/3	X = 1/2	X = 1/3	X = 1/4	X = 1/2	X = 1/4	X = 1/3	X = 1/2
						Priority	Priority	Priority	Priority	Priority	Priority	Priority	Priority	Priority
X1 = 11y/63	0.2381	0.4850	0.6402											
X2 = 5z/7	0.2381	0.2381	0.2381											
X3 = (2y−9z)/7	−0.0390	0.3651	0.6190											
X4 = 2z−y/9	0.5152	0.3580	0.2593											
X5 = (y/7 + z)/2	0.2641	0.3651	0.4286											
S1						**0.0759**	0.0831	0.0953	**0.0749**	0.0814	0.092	**0.0727**	0.0788	0.0886
S2						0.508	0.5167	0.5263	0.5788	0.5871	0.5955	0.6184	0.6256	0.6326
S3						**0.0788**	0.0792	0.0794	**0.0759**	0.0768	0.0777	**0.0727**	0.0739	0.0752
S4						0.3374	0.321	0.2991	0.2704	0.2547	0.2348	0.2362	0.2217	0.2035

Note: The rank reversal of S1 and S3 occurred in three places where two or one the left boundary values of variables are used, namely, x = 1/4 and y = 1; x = 1/4 and y = 1; x = 1/4 and y = 3

Table 6.7 The sensitivity analysis of rank reversal when the values of variable z is fixed (z = 1/2)

z = 1/2	Y = 45z/11	Y = 25z/3	Y = 11z	Y = 2, X = 1/3	Y = 2, X = 1	Y = 3, X = 1/3	Y = 3, X = 1	Y = 4, X = 1/3	Y = 4, X = 1	Y = 5, X = 1/3	Y = 5, X = 1	Y = 6, X = 1/3	Y = 6, X = 1
(2 ≤ Y ≤ 6, 1/3 ≤ X ≤ 1)	2.0455	4.1667	5.5000	Priority	Priority	Priority	Priority	Priority	Priority	Priority	Priority	Priority	Priority
X1 = 11y/63	0.3571	0.7275	0.9603										
X2 = 5z/7	0.3571	0.3571	0.3571										
X3 = (2y−9z)/7	−0.0584	0.5476	0.9286										
X4 = 2z−y/9	0.7727	0.5370	0.3889										
X5 = (y/7 + z)/2	0.3961	0.5476	0.6429										
S1				**0.0819**	0.1136	**0.0798**	0.1089	**0.0776**	0.105	**0.0755**	0.1017	**0.0736**	0.0989
S2				0.5966	0.6131	0.6334	0.6472	0.6587	0.6699	0.6781	0.6869	0.6939	0.7005
S3				**0.0868**	0.0866	**0.0832**	0.0843	**0.08**	0.0821	**0.0772**	0.0801	**0.0747**	0.0782
S4				0.2347	0.1867	0.2037	0.1596	0.1838	0.143	0.1692	0.1313	0.1579	0.1224

Note: The rank reversal of S1 and S3 occurred in five places where two groups of the boundary values of variables are used, That is, x = 1/3 and y = 2 ; x = 1/3 and y = 3 ; x = 1/3 and y = 4 ; x = 1/3 and y = 5 ; x = 1/3 and y = 6

Table 6.8 The sensitivity analysis of rank reversal when the values of variable z is fixed (z = 1)

z = 1	Y = 45z/11	Y = 25z/3	Y = 11z	4 ≤ Y ≤ 9	1/2 ≤ X ≤ 1
(z = 1)	4.0909	8.3333	11.0000	1.9206	
X1 = 11y/63	0.7143	1.4550	1.9206	0.7143	
X2 = 5z/7	0.7143	0.7143	0.7143	0.7143	
X3 = (2y−9z)/7	−0.1169	1.0951	1.8571		
X4 = 2z−y/9	1.5499	1.0741	0.7778		
X5 = (y/7 + z)/2	0.7922	1.0952	1.285		

Priority	Y = 4		Y = 5		Y = 6		Y = 7		Y = 8		Y = 9	
	X = 1/2	X = 1	X = 1/2	X = 1	X = 1/2	X = 1	X = 1/2	X = 1	X = 1/2	X = 1	X = 1/2	X = 1
S1	**0.0865**	0.1029	**0.0847**	0.1003	**0.0830**	0.0981	**0.0814**	0.0961	**0.0798**	0.0942	**0.0784**	0.0925
S2	0.6717	0.6789	0.6884	0.6947	0.7018	0.7072	0.7131	0.7175	0.7228	0.7264	0.7314	0.7341
S3	**0.0988**	0.0976	**0.0955**	0.0949	**0.0926**	0.0925	**0.09**	0.0904	**0.0877**	0.0885	**0.0855**	0.0867
S4	0.1429	0.1207	0.1314	0.1102	0.1226	0.1023	0.1155	0.0961	0.1097	0.091	0.1047	0.0867

Note: The rank reversal of S1 and S3 occurred in six places where, x = 1/2 and y = 4; x = 1/2 and y = 5; x = 1/2 and y = 6; x = 1/2 and y = 7; x = 1/2 and y = 8; x = 1/2 and y = 9

Table 6.9 The reversal points that cause rank reversal in S1 and S3

z	1/7	1/6	1/4	1/3	1/2	1
x	1/9	1/8	1/5	1/4	1/3	1/2
y	1/2	1/2, 1	1	1,2,3	2,3,4,5,6	4,5,6,7,8,9

Ranges of x and y variables when z is fixed:
$z = 1/7$: $1/9 \leq x \leq 1/4$; $1/2 \leq y \leq 2$ $z = 1/3$: $1/4 \leq x \leq 1/2$; $1 \leq y \leq 4$
$z = 1/6$: $1/8 \leq x \leq 1/4$; $1/2 \leq y \leq 2$ $z = 1/2$: $1/3 \leq x \leq 1$; $2 \leq y \leq 6$
$z = 1/4$: $1/5 \leq x \leq 1/3$; $1 \leq y \leq 3$ $z = 1$: $1/2 \leq x \leq 1$; $4 \leq y \leq 9$
Note that different levels of z values are chosen based on $1/7 < z < 1$ constraint, derived from Eq. (6.6)

Table 6.2 shows that when $z = 1/5$, variables x and y can be determined using Eqs. (6.3)–(6.4). The feasible regions within the 9-point scale are found to be: $1 \leq y \leq 2$ and $1/7 \leq x \leq 1/3$. We next perform the sensitivity analysis of rank reversal based on these ranges. The priorities of the four alternatives are derived and shown in Table 6.2. We found that the ranks of S1 and S3 are reversed in two places where two groups of the boundary values of variables are used. That is, $S1 = 0.0624 < S3 = 0.0644$ when $x = 1/7$ and $y = 1$; and $S1 = 0.0615 < S3 = 0.0620$ when $x = 1/7$ and $y = 2$. Likewise, the sensitivity analyses shown in Tables 6.3, 6.4, 6.5, 6.6, 6.7, and 6.8 are conducted by fixing the z value at a time. Table 6.9 summarizes the reversal points that cause rank reversal in S1 and S3.

From Tables 6.2 and 6.9, we found that rank reversal of S1 and S3 occur when both x and y variables reach the lower bound of the inequality constraints simultaneously, once the value of z is determined. When the x variable reaches the lower bound, and the values of y are within the ranges specified, rank reversal may also occur. Thus, whether the ranks of S1 and S3 will reverse depends on the inequality constraints of x and y once z is given. This will be also true when we fix x or y instead of z.

But why the ranks of S1 and S3 reverse when both x and y variables reach the lower bounds of their inequality constraints? Recall that to maintain the global consistency, we have to minimize the deviations in the induced bias matrix C. In the above S example, the weight of S1 is 0.1049, which is close to $S3 = 0.0965$. When the new S4 is added and the value of z is chosen, the importance between S3 and S4 is automatically determined by z. The feasible regions within the 9-point scale on both x and y variables can also be determined through matrix C.

In our example, for S1 and S3 to reverse the rank, the priority of S3 needs to be higher than that of S1. Since the importance between S3 and S4 is bounded by z, the importance of S3 can be improved by raising the weight of S4. Hence for rank reversal to take place between S1 and S3, we can increase the weight of S4 with respect to S1 and S2. Note that when both x and y reach their lower bounds, we know from the comparison matrix that S4 will be more important than S1 and S2. S4 has higher weight than S1 and S2; so is S3. Thus S3 has higher priority than S1 and rank reversal occurs. In summary, by identifying the boundary values of the inequality constraints on x and y given z, the proposed model can effectively perform sensitivity analysis to predict when rank reversal will take place.

References

Belton V, Gear T (1983) On a short-coming of Saaty's method of analytic hierarchies. Omega 11:228–230

Ergu D, Kou G, Peng Y, Shang J (2011g) A modular paradigm for the formation of the ANP structure: an integrated framework for supplier selection. Working paper, 2011

Millet I, Saaty TL (2000) On the relativity of relative measures – accommodating both rank preservation and rank reversal in the AHP. Eur J Oper Res 121(1):205–212

Saaty TL (2001b) Deriving the AHP 1–9 scale from first principles. In: ISAHP 2001 proceedings, Bern, Switzerland

Saaty TL, Vargas LG (1993) Experiments on rank preservation and reversal in relative measurement. Math Comput Model 17(4/5):13–18

Triantaphyllou E (2004) Two new cases of rank reversals when the AHP and some of its additive variants are used that do not occur with the multiplicative AHP. J Multi-Crit Decis Anal 10: 11–25

Wijnmalen DJD, Wedley WC (2008) Non-discriminating criteria in the AHP: removal and rank reversal. J Multi-Crit Decis Anal 15:143–149. doi:10.1002/mcda.430

Chapter 7
Applications of IBMM

The AHP and ANP are two of the widely used MCDM methods, and have been extensively applied to the real-world decision making problems. However, the inconsistency issue and missing item scores issue are still two of the major issues when AHP and ANP are used. In the previous Chapters, the IBMM is proposed to deal with the inconsistency issue, missing item scores, and rank reversal issue. In this Chapter, the IBMM is applied to two real world applications, the Task Scheduling and Resource Allocation in Cloud Computing Environment by AHP and Risk Assessment and Decision Analysis by ANP. Details are presented in Sects. 7.1 and 7.2.

7.1 Task Scheduling and Resource Allocation in Cloud Computing Environment by the IBMM

"A Cloud is a type of parallel and distributed system consisting of a collection of interconnected and virtualized computers that are dynamically provisioned and presented as one or more unified computing resources based on service-level agreements established through negotiation between the service provider and consumers." (Buyya et al. 2009). The computing resources, either software or hardware, are virtualized and allocated as services from providers to users. The computing resources can be allocated dynamically upon the requirements and preferences of consumers.

Traditional system-centric resource management architecture cannot process the resource assignment task and dynamically allocate the available resources in cloud computing environment. Fujiwara et al. (2009) proposed a market-based mechanism to allocate resources in a cloud computing environment, where the resources are virtualized and delivered to users as services. Since the consumers may access applications and data of the "Cloud" from anywhere at any time, it is difficult for the cloud service providers to allocate the cloud resources dynamically and efficiently.

G. Kou et al., *Data Processing for the AHP/ANP*, Quantitative Management 1,
DOI 10.1007/978-3-642-29213-2_7, © Springer-Verlag Berlin Heidelberg 2013

In Ergu et al. (2011e), a task-oriented resource allocation model is proposed. The tasks provided by the users are ranked by reciprocal pairwise comparison matrix and the Analytic Hierarchy Process (AHP). The cloud resources are assigned for the tasks according to the weight of each task determined by reciprocal pairwise comparison matrix of user preferences. Since different users could have conflicting preferences, there might be inconsistent elements in the reciprocal pairwise comparison matrix, thus the IBMM is used to improve the consistency ratio. Details are described as follows.

7.1.1 Resource Allocation in Cloud Computing

Resource allocation is a hot topic and key factor in distributed computing and grid computing (Huang and Chao 2001; Ismail et al. 2008; Wei et al. 2009; Moschakis and Karatza 2010). For distributed computing, processing capacity resources are homogeneous and reserved. However, for grid computing, the resources are highly unpredictable. The computers are heterogeneous, their capacities are typically unknown and changing over time, which may connect and disconnect from the grid at any time. Therefore, the same task is sent to more than one computer in Grid computing, and the user receives the output of the computer that completes the task first (Koole and Righter 2007). Dynamic allocation of tasks to computers is complicated in grid computing environment due to the complicated process of assigning multiple copies of the same task to different computers. Likewise, the resource allocation is also a big challenge in cloud computing.

Cloud computing not only enables users to migrate their data and computation to a remote location with minimal impact on system performance, but also easily access to cloud computing environment to visit their data and obtain the computation at anytime and anywhere (Hayes 2008). Cloud computing is attempting to provide cheap and easy access to measurable and billable computational resources comparing with other paradigms such as distribute computing, Grid computing etc. Therefore, Yazır et al. (2010) proposed a new approach for dynamic autonomous resource allocation in computing clouds through distributed multiple criteria decision analysis. In cloud computing environment, the tasks are distributed across distinct computational nodes. In order to allocate cloud computing resources, nodes with spare computing power are detected, and network bandwidth, line quality, response time, task costs, and reliability of resource allocation are analyzed. Hence, the quality of cloud computing service can be described by resources such as network bandwidth, complete time, task costs, and reliability etc. The framework of task scheduling and resource allocation in cloud computing environment is shown in Fig. 7.1.

In the proposed framework, computing tasks are collected in Task Pool. Tasks are ranked and submitted to computing resources distributed in Cloud Computing Nodes. The computing resources are allocated according to the weights of tasks. The proposed framework will be further illustrated in the following section.

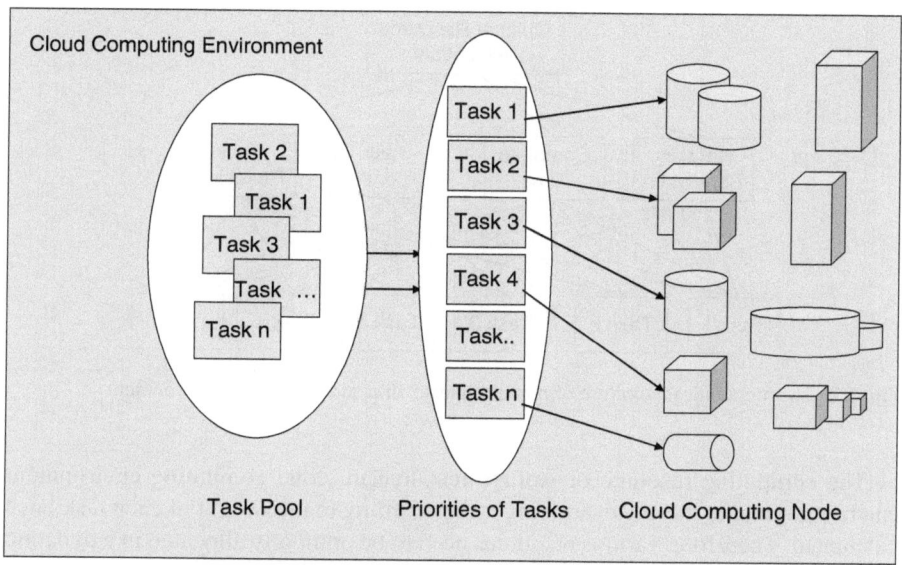

Fig. 7.1 Task scheduling and resource allocation in cloud computing environment

7.1.2 Task-Oriented Resource Allocation in Cloud Computing

In order to efficiently allocate computing resources, scheduling becomes a very complicated task in cloud computing environment where many alternative computers with varying capacities are available. Efficient task scheduling mechanism can meet users' requirements and improve the resource utilization (Fang et al. 2010). The cloud service providers often receive lots of computing requests with different requirements and preferences from users simultaneously. Some tasks need to be fulfilled at lower cost and less computing resources, while some tasks require higher computing ability and take more bandwidth and computing resources. To improve the utility of resource and meet users' requirements, all tasks should be ranked according to available resources such as network bandwidth, complete time, task costs, and reliability of task, which can be structured in a hierarchy as shown in Fig. 7.2.

When the cloud computing service providers receive the tasks from users, the tasks can be pairwise compared using the comparison matrix technique. The cloud computing providers negotiate with the users on the requirements of tasks including network bandwidth, complete time, task costs, and reliability of task. A comparison matrix can be built based on the Saaty Rating Scale (Saaty 1990) as shown in Table 2.2, which is used to determine the relative importance of each task in terms of each criterion. The weights of all tasks can be derived using the analysis hierarchy process (AHP).

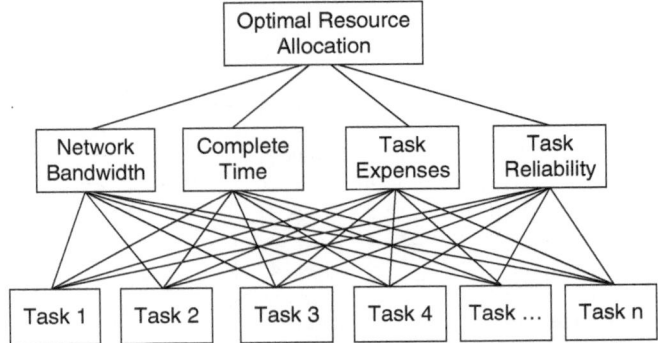

Fig. 7.2 The hierarchical structure of requested tasks in cloud computing environment

The computing resource or storage resource in cloud computing environment can be assigned to the corresponding task according to the weight of each task once calculated. Therefore, various resources need to be optimally allocated in a dynamic setting in terms of the weights of tasks to maximize the cloud computing system performance.

7.1.3 Illustrative Examples

When the CR is more than 0.1, the reciprocal comparison matrix needs to be adjusted until the CR is less than 0.1. Saaty has proved that the final priority vectors remain the same as long as the CR is less than 0.1, therefore in most cases, a reciprocal comparison matrix is valid if the CR is less than 0.1. However, it is different for tasks priorities in cloud computing since the computing resources are allocated according to the weights of the requested tasks, and the charges are also paid in terms of what kinds of computing resources are used to fulfill the tasks. To illustrate the strict consistency requirement for tasks which computing resources should be allocated, two examples with four requested tasks and with eight requested tasks are used in the following.

Example 7.1. Assume there are four tasks applying for the cloud computing resource, the comparison matrix with respect to the response time is:

Response time	T1	T2	T3	T4	Priorities
T1	1	4	2	6	0.5301
T2	$\frac{1}{4}$	1	2	4	0.2339
T3	$\frac{1}{2}$	$\frac{1}{2}$	1	2	0.1643
T4	$\frac{1}{6}$	$\frac{1}{4}$	$\frac{1}{2}$	1	0.0716
CR $= 0.0736$					

In order to present explicitly, the comparison matrix is denoted as

$$
A = \begin{bmatrix} 1 & 4 & 2 & 6 \\ \dfrac{1}{4} & 1 & 2 & 4 \\ \dfrac{1}{2} & \dfrac{1}{2} & 1 & 2 \\ \dfrac{1}{6} & \dfrac{1}{4} & \dfrac{1}{2} & 1 \end{bmatrix}
$$

Apply the proposed consistency identification method to further improve the consistency ratio.

Step 1: The induced matrix $C = A * A - 4 * A$ is

$$
C = \begin{bmatrix} 0 & -5.5 & 7 & 8 \\ 1.1667 & 0 & -1.5 & -2.5 \\ -0.5417 & 1.5 & 0 & 1 \\ -0.0208 & 0.4167 & -0.1667 & 0 \end{bmatrix}
$$

Step 2: The largest value in matrix C is 8, where location is 1st row and 4th column.

Step 3: Identify all the values in 1st row and 4th column of pair-wise matrix A, that is

$$
r_1 = \begin{pmatrix} 1 & 4 & 2 & 6 \end{pmatrix}, \text{ and } c_4^T = \begin{pmatrix} 6 & 4 & 2 & 1 \end{pmatrix}
$$

Step 4: The scalar product b of the vectors r_1 and c_4^T in the dimension 4, that is

$$
b = r_1 \cdot c_4^T = \begin{pmatrix} 6 & 16 & 4 & 6 \end{pmatrix}
$$

Step 5: The bias identifying vector f is

$$
f = b - a_{14} = \begin{pmatrix} 0 & 10 & -2 & 0 \end{pmatrix}
$$

Step 6: The value, 10, is the largest one far from zero, and others are zero or close to zero. It indicates that $a_{14} = 6$ is probably correct while $10 = a_{12}a_{24} - a_{14}$ is the inconsistent element. $a_{12}a_{24}$ may have problem.

Step 7: As $c_{12} = -5.5 < 0$ and $c_{24} = -2.5 < 0$, the corresponding elements a_{12} and a_{24} are too large.

Suppose the a_{12} is decreased to 2, then the revised comparison matrix A becomes:

$$
A = \begin{bmatrix}
1 & 2 & 2 & 6 \\
\dfrac{1}{2} & 1 & 2 & 4 \\
\dfrac{1}{2} & \dfrac{1}{2} & 1 & 2 \\
\dfrac{1}{6} & \dfrac{1}{4} & \dfrac{1}{2} & 1
\end{bmatrix}
$$

Calculate the eigenvector and eigenvalue of matrix A as well as the consistency ratio, we get

$$\lambda_{max} = 4.0458, \quad and \quad C.I. = 0.89$$

$$C.R. = \frac{(\lambda_{max} - n)/(n-1)}{R.I.} = \frac{(\lambda_{max} - 4)/3}{0.89} = \frac{(4.0458 - 4)/3}{0.89} = 0.0172 < 0.1$$

The eigenvector with respect to the maximum eigenvalue is shown below.

Response time	T1	T2	T3	T4	Priorities
T1	1	2	2	6	0.4578
T2	$\frac{1}{2}$	1	2	4	0.2910
T3	$\frac{1}{2}$	$\frac{1}{2}$	1	2	0.1738
T4	$\frac{1}{6}$	$\frac{1}{4}$	$\frac{1}{2}$	1	0.0775
CR = 0.0172					

Compare the final priorities of four tasks with respect to response time with CR = 0.0736 and CR = 0.0172 respectively, which is shown as follows,

Tasks	CR = 0.0736 Priorities	CR = 0.0172 Priorities
T1	0.5301	0.4578
T2	0.2339	0.2910
T3	0.1643	0.1738
T4	0.0716	0.0775

It is shown that the weight of task 1 decreases, and the weights of task 2, task 3 and task 4 increase slightly. Although the ranking results do not change, the weights of tasks have changed. In the cloud computing resource allocation, there are massive computers linked together to executive the corresponding tasks with different preferences and requirement. The tasks with different weights will be assigned to different cloud computing nodes, which may lead to different computing resources usages and expenses. Therefore, the further inconsistency identification even the CR is already less than 0.1 is becoming important and meaningful.

From the revised comparison matrix A, there still have some inconsistent judgments, such as $a_{13}a_{34} = 4 \neq a_{14} = 6$ and $a_{12}a_{24} = 8 \neq a_{14} = 6$, although the CR is equal to 0.0172. In order to further improve the consistency ratio, the induced bias matrix again can be used to identify the inconsistent elements.

Step 1: The induced matrix $C = A * A - 4 * A$ is

$$C = \begin{bmatrix} 0 & -1.5 & 3 & 0 \\ 0.66 & 0 & -1 & -1 \\ -0.416 & 0.5 & 0 & 1 \\ 0.041 & 0.0833 & -0.166 & 0 \end{bmatrix}$$

Step 2: The largest value in matrix C is 3, where location is 1st row and 3rd column.
Step 3: Draw out all the values in 1st row and 3rd column of pair-wise matrix A, that is

$$r_1 = \begin{pmatrix} 1 & 2 & 2 & 6 \end{pmatrix}, \text{ and } c_3^T = \begin{pmatrix} 2 & 2 & 1 & 1/2 \end{pmatrix}$$

Step 4: The scalar product b of the vectors r_1 and c_3^T in the dimension 4, that is

$$b = r_1 \cdot c_3^T = \begin{pmatrix} 2 & 4 & 2 & 3 \end{pmatrix}$$

Step 5: The bias identifying vector f is

$$f = b - a_{13} = \begin{pmatrix} 0 & 2 & 0 & 1 \end{pmatrix}$$

Step 6: The values, 2, is the largest one. Because $2 = a_{12}a_{23} - a_{13}$, it shows that a_{13} might be slightly small or the elements a_{12}, a_{23}, may be slightly large.
Step 7: As $c_{13} = 3 > 0$, $c_{12} = -1.5 < 0$, $c_{23} = -1 < 0$, the corresponding element a_{13} is too small, the corresponding elements a_{12}, a_{23}, are too large. The method of matrix order reduction (Ergu et al. 2011b) is applied to identify the elements a_{13}, a_{12}, a_{23}. When the task 1 was removed from the matrix A, namely, the first row and first column are deleted, the induced matrix C becomes:

$$\begin{pmatrix} 0 & 0 & 0 \\ 0 & 0 & 0 \\ 0 & 0 & 0 \end{pmatrix}$$

It shows that the inconsistent elements are a_{12}, a_{13}, namely, a_{13} is too small and a_{12} is too large. It explains that both of the elements have affected $c_{14} = 0$.

The results of the identification explain the reasons why the following inequalities occur. That is,

$$\text{Since } a_{13} \text{ is too small, } a_{13}a_{34} = 4 < a_{14} = 6$$
$$\text{Since } a_{12} \text{ is too large, } a_{12}a_{24} = 8 > a_{14} = 6$$

Suppose the a_{13} is increased to 3, and calculate the eigenvalue, consistency ratio and eigenvector for the second revised comparison matrix, we can get

$$\lambda_{max} = 4.0104, \quad CR = 0.0039, \quad W = (0.4899\ 0.2827\ 0.1516\ 0.0758).$$

The weights of task 1 increased from 0.4578 to 0.4899 while the weights of task 3 decreased from 0.1738 to 0.1516. The weights of task 2 and task 4 changed slightly.

Example 7.2. To further illustrate the importance of inconsistency identification under $CR < 0.1$ in cloud computing resource allocation, we take the comparison matrix in eight order (Ergu et al. 2011b) as an example. Assume there are eight tasks applying for the cloud computing resources, and the comparison matrix with respect to task expenses and the priorities of all tasks are listed below

Task expenses	T1	T2	T3	T4	T5	T6	T7	T8	Priorities
T1	1	2	1/2	2	1/2	2	1/2	2	0.1091
T2	1/2	1	4	1	1/4	1	1/4	1	0.1238
T3	2	1/4	1	4	1	4	1	4	0.1669
T4	1/2	1	1/4	1	1/4	1	1/4	1	0.0546
T5	2	4	1	4	1	4	1	4	0.2183
T6	1/2	1	1/4	1	1/4	1	1/4	1	0.0546
T7	2	4	1	4	1	4	1	4	0.2183
T8	1/2	1	1/4	1	1/4	1	1/4	1	0.0546
CR = 0.1055									

The inconsistent values in the comparison matrix are identified by the IBMM model (Ergu et al. 2011b), namely, a_{32} is too small while a_{23} is too large. Let us assume the a_{32} is increased to 1/3 from 1/4, and a_{23} is decreased to 3 from 4, then calculate the corresponding CR and priority vectors of tasks, we get:

Task expenses	T1	T2	T3	T4	T5	T6	T7	T8	Priorities
T1	1	2	1/2	2	1/2	2	1/2	2	0.1114
T2	1/2	1	3	1	1/4	1	1/4	1	0.0933
T3	2	1/3	1	4	1	4	1	4	0.1825
T4	1/2	1	1/4	1	1/4	1	1/4	1	0.0557
T5	2	4	1	4	1	4	1	4	0.2228
T6	1/2	1	1/4	1	1/4	1	1/4	1	0.0557
T7	2	4	1	4	1	4	1	4	0.2228
T8	1/2	1	1/4	1	1/4	1	1/4	1	0.0557
CR = 0.0504									

Further change a_{32} to 4 from 1/4, and a_{23} to 1/4, and calculate the CR and priority weights of all tasks, we get

Task expenses	T1	T2	T3	T4	T5	T6	T7	T8	Priorities
T1	1	2	1/2	2	1/2	2	1/2	2	0.1111
T2	1/2	1	1/4	1	1/4	1	1/4	1	0.0556
T3	2	4	1	4	1	4	1	4	0.2222
T4	1/2	1	1/4	1	1/4	1	1/4	1	0.0556
T5	2	4	1	4	1	4	1	4	0.2222
T6	1/2	1	1/4	1	1/4	1	1/4	1	0.0556
T7	2	4	1	4	1	4	1	4	0.2222
T8	1/2	1	1/4	1	1/4	1	1/4	1	0.0556
CR = 0.000									

The comparison of priority weights for eight tasks with different acceptable CR is shown below.

Tasks	CR = 0.1055	CR = 0.0504	CR = 0
T1	0.1091	0.1114	0.1111
T2	0.1238	0.0933	0.0556
T3	0.1669	0.1825	0.2222
T4	0.0546	0.0557	0.0556
T5	0.2183	0.2228	0.2222
T6	0.0546	0.0557	0.0556
T7	0.2183	0.2228	0.2222
T8	0.0546	0.0557	0.0556

When the CR = 0.1055, the weights of task 5 and task 7 both are 0.2183, the weight of task 3 is 0.1669, while the weights of task 2 and task 1, are 0.1238 and 0.1091, respectively. However, the weights of task 4, task 6, and task 8 are identical, 0.0546.

When the CR is decreased to 0.0504, the weights of task 5 and task 7 both increased to 0.2228. The weight of task 3 also increased to 0.1825, and the weight of task 1 increased slightly to 0.1114. However, the weight of task 2 decreased to 0.0933. The weights of task 4, task 6, and task 8 increased slightly to 0.0557 from 0.0546.

When the CR is decreased to 0, namely, the comparison matrix is completely consistent. The priority weights have been changed. The weights of task 3, task 5, and task 7 become 0.2222, the weights of task 2, task 4, and task 6 are 0.0556, and the weight of task 1 is 0.1111.

Therefore, the computing resource allocation will be different for the tasks under different consistency ratios.

7.2 Risk Assessment and Decision Analysis by the IBMM

7.2.1 Background of Risk Assessment and Decision Analysis

Over the past few decades, risk assessment and decision analysis has been an active research area (For instance: Reckhow 1994; Bonano et al. 2000; Hämäläinen et al. 2000; Khadam and Kaluarachchi 2003; Linkov et al. 2006; Krewski et al. 2009; Wagner et al. 2009; Peng et al. 2008, 2011a, b, c). The decision analysts have to make quick and efficient decision for multi-criteria decision making (MCDM) problems such as identifying the key factors of the risk and the potential risk, determining risk level and risk consequences, analyzing the uncertain variables of a decision, and considering different preferences etc. For instance, the emergency managers have to select emergency prevention alternatives, emergency pre-response plans, emergency response alternatives, and emergency recovery alternatives (Hu et al. 2007).

The AHP (analytical hierarchy process), as a widely used MCDM method, is often implemented in the Benefit – Opportunity – Cost – Risk (BOCR) analysis to improve the effectiveness of risk assessment and decision analysis (Wijnmalen 2007; Saaty 2008; Aguilar-Lasserre et al. 2009; Saaty and Zoffer 2011). However, in reality, risk assessment and decision analysis problems are often too complicated to be structured hierarchically. Therefore, the analytical network process (ANP) is widely used to assess the key factors of risks and analyze the impacts and preferences of decision alternatives. When the ANP is applied to assess and analyze the factors of the existing risk and potential risks as well as the impacts of a decision for an emergent event, the consistency of the comparison matrix and the inconsistent elements should be identified and adjusted as soon as possible. The risk assessment and decision analysis of an emergent event is a typical time-critical information service which is highly dependent on time and information. To improve the efficiency of response decision making in risk assessment and decision analysis, in Ergu et al. (2011a, d), a maximum eigenvalue threshold index method is proposed as the new consistency index for the ANP. A bias block diagonal matrix consists of the inconsistent comparison matrices is introduced to rapidly identify and adjust the inconsistent elements in the original inconsistent comparison matrices when the ANP is applied to the risk assessment and decision analysis.

7.2.2 Illustrative Examples

To further illustrate the maximum eigenvalue threshold index and the induced bias block matrix as described in Chap. 2 for rapidly identifying the inconsistent

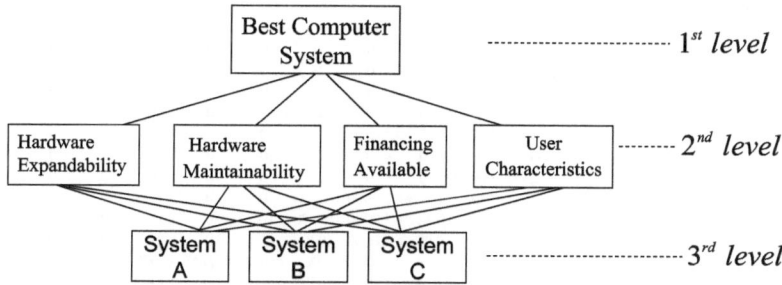

Fig. 7.3 The structure of selecting the best computer system

elements of the comparison matrices when the ANP is applied in risk assessment, decision analysis and emergency management, two public-domain examples are revised to test the proposed method.

Example 7.3. With the development of the information communication technology (ICT), the computer system (CS) is increasingly important and becoming one of the central components in risk assessment and decision analysis. However, CS is not reliable in emergent events such as earthquake, fire emergence even stolen/Hi-jack. In such scenarios, the emergency managers have to select the most reliable computer system. The example first introduced by Triantaphyllou and Mann (1995) and used in Chap. 2, is again used to illustrate the proposed method. The structure of this example is shown in Fig. 7.3. Suppose there are three alternative configurations, system A, system B, and system C. There are also four criteria, hardware expandability, hardware maintainability, financing available, and user friendly characteristics of the operating system and related available software, denoted as C1, C2, C3, and C4 respectively.

Since the Gradual-level consistency test and inconsistency identification method is relatively simple compared with the Whole-Level Method, therefore, the whole level method is used to test the consistency and identify the inconsistent elements in this example. The whole process can be divided into two stages, consistency test and inconsistency identification.

Stage I: Test the consistency of all the comparison matrices using whole-level method.

Step 1: Construct the block diagonal matrix B showed below using the matrices A, C1, C2, C3 and C4.

Columns 1 through 11   *Columns 12 through 16*

```
Columns 1 through 11                                                         Columns 12 through 16
1.0000 5.0000 3.0000 7.0000    0      0      0      0      0      0      0        0      0      0      0      0
0.2000 1.0000 0.3333 5.0000    0      0      0      0      0      0      0        0      0      0      0      0
0.3333 3.0000 1.0000 6.0000    0      0      0      0      0      0      0        0      0      0      0      0
0.1429 0.2000 0.1667 1.0000    0      0      0      0      0      0      0        0      0      0      0      0
   0      0      0      0   1.0000 6.0000 8.0000    0      0      0      0        0      0      0      0      0
   0      0      0      0   0.1667 1.0000 4.0000    0      0      0      0        0      0      0      0      0
   0      0      0      0   0.1250 0.2500 1.0000    0      0      0      0        0      0      0      0      0
   0      0      0      0      0      0      0   1.0000 7.0000 0.2000    0        0      0      0      0      0
   0      0      0      0      0      0      0   0.1429 1.0000 0.1250    0        0      0      0      0      0
   0      0      0      0      0      0      0   5.0000 8.0000 1.0000    0        0      0      0      0      0
   0      0      0      0      0      0      0      0      0      0   1.0000    8.0000 6.0000    0      0      0
   0      0      0      0      0      0      0      0      0      0   0.1250    1.0000 0.2500    0      0      0
   0      0      0      0      0      0      0      0      0      0   0.1667    4.0000 1.0000    0      0      0
   0      0      0      0      0      0      0      0      0      0      0        0      0   1.0000 5.0000 4.0000
   0      0      0      0      0      0      0      0      0      0      0        0      0   0.2000 1.0000 0.3333
   0      0      0      0      0      0      0      0      0      0      0        0      0   0.2500 3.0000 1.0000
```

Step 2: Calculate the eigenvalue of block diagonal matrix B, and identify the maximum eigenvalues of the corresponding block diagonal sub-matrix A, C1, C2, C3 and C4. That is:

$$\lambda^0_{max} = 4.2365, \quad \lambda^1_{max} = 3.1356, \quad \lambda^2_{max} = 3.2470, \quad \lambda^3_{max} = 3.1356,$$

$$\lambda^4_{max} = 3.0858$$

Step 3: Test the consistency using the maximum eigenvalue threshold method. That is:

$$\Delta\lambda^i_{max} = \left(\lambda^0_{max}, \lambda^1_{max}, \lambda^2_{max}, \lambda^3_{max}, \lambda^4_{max}\right) - \left(\lambda^4_{max\,thrd}, \lambda^3_{max\,thrd}, \lambda^3_{max\,thrd}, \lambda^3_{max\,thrd}, \lambda^3_{max\,thrd}\right)$$

$$= (3.1356, \ 3.2470, \ 3.1356, \ 3.0858) - (4.267, \ 3.104, \ 3.104, 3.104, 3.104)$$

$$= (-0.0305, \ 0.0316, \ 0.143, \ 0.0316, -0.0182)$$

Obviously, only $\Delta\lambda^0_{max} < 0$ and $\Delta\lambda^4_{max} < 0$, which mean only the two comparison matrices A and $C4$ are consistent, and other matrices are inconsistent.

Stage II: Identify the inconsistent elements using the whole level identification principal.

Step 1: Construct the whole block matrix B using all the inconsistent matrices C1, C2 and C3.

```
1.0000 6.0000 8.0000    0      0      0      0      0      0
0.1667 1.0000 4.0000    0      0      0      0      0      0
0.1250 0.2500 1.0000    0      0      0      0      0      0
   0      0      0   1.0000 7.0000 0.2000    0      0      0
   0      0      0   0.1429 1.0000 0.1250    0      0      0
   0      0      0   5.0000 8.0000 1.0000    0      0      0
   0      0      0      0      0      0   1.0000 8.0000 6.0000
   0      0      0      0      0      0   0.1250 1.0000 0.2500
   0      0      0      0      0      0   0.1667 4.0000 1.0000
```

Step 2:   Introduce the whole induced bias block matrix using the formula $C = BB - 3B$. That is

0	−4.0000	16.0000	0	0	0	0	0	0
0.3333	0	−2.6667	0	0	0	0	0	0
−0.0833	0.5000	0	0	0	0	0	0	0
0	0	0	0	−5.4000	0.6750	0	0	0
0	0	0	0.4821	0	−0.0964	0	0	0
0	0	0	−3.8571	27.0000	0	0	0	0
0	0	0	0	0	0	0	16.0000	−4.0000
0	0	0	0	0	0	−0.0833	0	0.5000
0	0	0	0	0	0	0.3333	−2.6667	0

Step 3: The largest values, 16, 27 and 16 in each sub-matrix, are located at 1st row and 3rd column, 6th row and 5th column, 7th row and 8th column, respectively.

Step 4: The corresponding vectors are

$$r_1 = \begin{pmatrix} 1 & 6 & 8 & 0 & 0 & 0 & 0 & 0 & 0 \end{pmatrix} \quad \text{and}$$

$$c_3^T = \begin{pmatrix} 8 & 4 & 1 & 0 & 0 & 0 & 0 & 0 & 0 \end{pmatrix}$$

$$r_6 = \begin{pmatrix} 0 & 0 & 0 & 5 & 8 & 1 & 0 & 0 & 0 \end{pmatrix} \quad \text{and}$$

$$c_5^T = \begin{pmatrix} 0 & 0 & 0 & 7 & 1 & 8 & 0 & 0 & 0 \end{pmatrix}$$

$$r_7 = \begin{pmatrix} 0 & 0 & 0 & 0 & 0 & 0 & 1 & 8 & 6 \end{pmatrix} \quad \text{and}$$

$$c_8^T = \begin{pmatrix} 0 & 0 & 0 & 0 & 0 & 0 & 8 & 1 & 4 \end{pmatrix}$$

Step 5: The corresponding scalar products b_i $(i = 1, 2, 3)$ are

$$b_1 = r_1 \cdot c_3^T = \begin{pmatrix} 8 & 24 & 8 & 0 & 0 & 0 & 0 & 0 & 0 \end{pmatrix}$$

$$b_2 = r_6 \cdot c_5^T = \begin{pmatrix} 0 & 0 & 0 & 35 & 8 & 8 & 0 & 0 & 0 \end{pmatrix}$$

$$b_3 = r_7 \cdot c_8^T = \begin{pmatrix} 0 & 0 & 0 & 0 & 0 & 0 & 8 & 8 & 24 \end{pmatrix}$$

Step 6: The corresponding bias identifying vectors f_i $(i = 1, 2, 3)$ are

$$f_1 = r_1 \cdot c_3^T - b_{13} = \begin{pmatrix} 0 & 16 & 0 & -8 & -8 & -8 & -8 & -8 & -8 \end{pmatrix}$$

$$f_2 = r_6 \cdot c_5^T - b_{65} = \begin{pmatrix} -8 & -8 & -8 & 27 & 0 & 0 & -8 & -8 & -8 \end{pmatrix}$$

$$f_3 = r_7 \cdot c_8^T - b_{78} = \begin{pmatrix} -8 & -8 & -8 & -8 & -8 & -8 & 0 & 0 & 16 \end{pmatrix}$$

Step 7: From the scalar products b_i $(i = 1, 2, 3)$ and the bias identifying vectors f_i $(i = 1, 2, 3)$, the inconsistent values are $b_{12}b_{23} = 24$, $b_{64}b_{45} = 35$ and $b_{79}b_{98} = 24$, which are corresponding the inconsistent elements $C1_{12}C1_{23} = 24$, $C2_{31}C2_{12} = 35$ and $C3_{13}C3_{32} = 24$.

Furthermore, $c_{12} = -4 < 0$, $c_{23} = -2.6667 < 0$, $c_{64} = -3.8571 < 0$, $c_{45} = -5.4 < 0$, $c_{79} = -4 < 0$ and $c_{98} = -2.6667 < 0$. These inequalities indicate that all values of $b_{12}, b_{23}, b_{64}, b_{45}, b_{79}$ and b_{98} are probably too large. That is, $C1_{12}, C1_{23}$, $C2_{31}, C2_{12}, C3_{13}$ and $C3_{32}$ are too large, and their values should be decreased. Namely, $C1_{12}C1_{23} = 8$, $C2_{31}C2_{12} = 8$ and $C3_{13}C3_{32} = 8$. For instance,

$$C1_{12} = 4, \ C1_{21} = \frac{1}{4} \quad C1_{23} = 2, \ C1_{32} = \frac{1}{2}$$

$$C2_{31} = 2, \ C2_{13} = \frac{1}{2} \quad C2_{12} = 4, \ C2_{21} = \frac{1}{4}$$

$$C3_{13} = 4, \ C3_{31} = \frac{1}{4} \quad C3_{32} = 2, \ C3_{23} = \frac{1}{2}$$

Then, the corresponding values in the comparison matrices C1, C2, and C3 are replaced with the above values, and reconstruct the block diagonal matrix B, which is shown as follows:

1.0000	4.0000	8.0000	0	0	0	0	0	0
0.2500	1.0000	2.0000	0	0	0	0	0	0
0.1250	0.5000	1.0000	0	0	0	0	0	0
0	0	0	1.0000	4.0000	0.5000	0	0	0
0	0	0	0.2500	1.0000	0.1250	0	0	0
0	0	0	2.0000	8.0000	1.0000	0	0	0
0	0	0	0	0	0	1.0000	8.0000	4.0000
0	0	0	0	0	0	0.1250	1.0000	0.5000
0	0	0	0	0	0	0.2500	2.0000	1.0000

The corresponding maximum values of the diagonal sub-matrices in the block diagonal matrix B can be calculated by calculating the eigenvalue of matrix B. Three of the maximum values are 3, which are equal to the order 3, therefore, they are consistent comparison matrices. We also can calculate the bias matrix C using the formula $C = BB - 3B$, which is listed below.

0	0	0	0	0	0	0	0	0
0	0	0	0	0	0	0	0	0
0	0	0	0	0	0	0	0	0
0	0	0	0	0	0	0	0	0
0	0	0	0	0	0	0	0	0
0	0	0	0	0	0	0	0	0
0	0	0	0	0	0	0	0	0
0	0	0	0	0	0	0	0	0
0	0	0	0	0	0	0	0	0

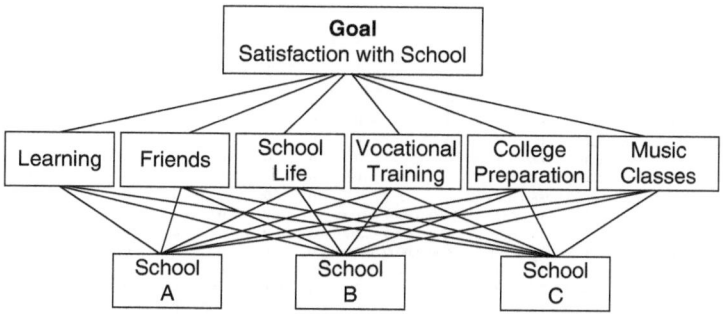

Fig. 7.4 The school choice hierarchy

Therefore, the consistencies of all the comparison matrices can easily be tested simultaneously by the proposed maximum eigenvalue index, and the inconsistent elements of the inconsistent comparison matrices can also be identified and adjusted simultaneously by the proposed Whole-level identification method.

Example 7.4. In Wenchuan Earthquake, many schools were destroyed. Survived students, especially high middle school students, have to transfer and select another school to continue their study. The ANP can be used to help the students selecting the best school. To further illustrate the proposed method in such scenario, the best school selection example first introduced by Saaty (1993) is used in this paper. In addition, this example was again used by Saaty (2008) to illustrate the ANP Formulation of the Classic AHP School Example. The school choice hierarchy is showed in Fig. 7.4. There are also six pairwise comparison matrices in this hierarchy structure. One with order six (6×6) with respect to the Goal, satisfaction with school, six comparison matrices with order three (3×3) with respect to the six criteria, Learning, Friends, School Life, Vocational Training, College Preparation and Music Classes, which are connected to the three alternatives.

The Whole-level consistency test and inconsistency identification methods have been illustrated in previous example, therefore, the Gradual-level method is used in this example to test the consistency and identify the inconsistent elements.

Stage I: Test the consistencies of all the comparison matrices using Gradual-level method.

Step 1: Construct the corresponding block diagonal matrix B_1 and B_2 showed below respectively using the matrix A in the first level, and the matrices C1, C2, C3, C4, C5, and C6 in the second level.

$$
\begin{array}{cccccc}
1.0000 & 4.0000 & 3.0000 & 1.0000 & 3.0000 & 4.0000 \\
0.2500 & 1.0000 & 7.0000 & 3.0000 & 0.2000 & 1.0000 \\
0.3333 & 0.1429 & 1.0000 & 0.2000 & 0.2000 & 0.1667 \\
1.0000 & 0.3333 & 5.0000 & 1.0000 & 1.0000 & 0.3333 \\
0.3333 & 5.0000 & 5.0000 & 1.0000 & 1.0000 & 3.0000 \\
0.2500 & 1.0000 & 6.0000 & 3.0000 & 0.3333 & 1.0000 \\
\end{array}
$$

and

Columns 1 through 11 · Columns 12 through 18

1.0000	0.3333	0.5000	0	0	0	0	0	0	0	0	0	0	0	0	0	0	0
3.0000	1.0000	3.0000	0	0	0	0	0	0	0	0	0	0	0	0	0	0	0
2.0000	0.3333	1.0000	0	0	0	0	0	0	0	0	0	0	0	0	0	0	0
0	0	0	1.0000	1.0000	1.0000	0	0	0	0	0	0	0	0	0	0	0	0
0	0	0	1.0000	1.0000	1.0000	0	0	0	0	0	0	0	0	0	0	0	0
0	0	0	1.0000	1.0000	1.0000	0	0	0	0	0	0	0	0	0	0	0	0
0	0	0	0	0	0	1.0000	5.0000	1.0000	0	0	0	0	0	0	0	0	0
0	0	0	0	0	0	0.2000	1.0000	0.2000	0.	0	0	0	0	0	0	0	0
0	0	0	0	0	0	1.0000	5.0000	1.0000	0	0	0	0	0	0	0	0	0
0	0	0	0	0	0	0	0	0	1.0000	9.0000	7.0000	0	0	0	0	0	0
0	0	0	0	0	0	0	0	0	0.1111	1.0000	0.2000	0	0	0	0	0	0
0	0	0	0	0	0	0	0	0	0.1429	5.0000	1.0000	0	0	0	0	0	0
0	0	0	0	0	0	0	0	0	0	0	0	1.0000	0.50000	1.0000	0	0	0
0	0	0	0	0	0	0	0	0	0	0	0	2.0000	1.0000	2.0000	0	0	0
0	0	0	0	0	0	0	0	0	0	0	0	1.0000	0.50000	1.0000	0	0	0
0	0	0	0	0	0	0	0	0	0	0	0	0	0	0	1.0000	6.0000	4.0000
0	0	0	0	0	0	0	0	0	0	0	0	0	0	0	0.1667	1.0000	0.3333
0	0	0	0	0	0	0	0	0	0	0	0	0	0	0	0.2500	3.0000	1.0000

Step 2: Calculate the maximum eigenvalues of block diagonal matrix B_1 and B_2, and identify the corresponding eigenvalues of comparison matrices A, C1, C2, C3, C4, C5, and C6, denoted as λ^i_{max} $(i = 0, 1, 2, \ldots, 6)$. We get $\lambda^0_{max} = 7.4199$ and

$$\lambda^1_{max} = 3.0536, \ \lambda^2_{max} = 3, \ \lambda^3_{max} = 3, \ \lambda^4_{max} = 3.2085, \lambda^5_{max} = 3,$$

$$\lambda^6_{max} = 3.0536$$

Step 3: Test the consistencies using the maximum eigenvalue threshold method. That is:

$$\Delta\lambda^0_{max} = \lambda^0_{max} - \lambda^6_{lim\,max} = 7.4199 - 6.781 = 0.6389 > 0$$

$$\Delta\lambda^i_{max} = (\lambda^1_{max}, \ \lambda^2_{max}, \ \lambda^3_{max}, \ \lambda^4_{max}, \ \lambda^5_{max}, \ \lambda^6_{max}) - \lambda^3_{lim\,max}$$

$$= (3.0536, \ 3, \ 3, \ 3.2085, \ 3, \ 3.0536) - 3.104$$

$$= (-0.0504, \ -0.1040, \ -0.1040, \ 0.1045, \ -0.1040, \ -0.0504)$$

Since $\Delta\lambda^0_{max} = 0.6389 > 0$ and $\Delta\lambda^4 = 0.1045 > 0$, therefore, the comparison matrix A and C4 are inconsistent. Go to the second stage. The whole-level identification method is used here, because there are only two inconsistent comparison matrices.

Stage II: Identify the inconsistent elements using the Whole-level identification principal.

Step 1: Construct the whole block matrix B using the inconsistent matrices A and C4.

$$
\begin{array}{ccccccccc}
1.0000 & 4.0000 & 3.0000 & 1.0000 & 3.0000 & 4.0000 & 0 & 0 & 0 \\
0.2500 & 1.0000 & 7.0000 & 3.0000 & 0.2000 & 1.0000 & 0 & 0 & 0 \\
0.3333 & 0.1429 & 1.0000 & 0.2000 & 0.2000 & 0.1667 & 0 & 0 & 0 \\
1.0000 & 0.3333 & 5.0000 & 1.0000 & 1.0000 & 0.3333 & 0 & 0 & 0 \\
0.3333 & 5.0000 & 5.0000 & 1.0000 & 1.0000 & 3.0000 & 0 & 0 & 0 \\
0.2500 & 1.0000 & 6.0000 & 3.0000 & 0.3333 & 1.0000 & 0 & 0 & 0 \\
0 & 0 & 0 & 0 & 0 & 0 & 1.0000 & 9.0000 & 7.0000 \\
0 & 0 & 0 & 0 & 0 & 0 & 0.1111 & 1.0000 & 0.2000 \\
0 & 0 & 0 & 0 & 0 & 0 & 0.1429 & 5.0000 & 1.0000
\end{array}
$$

Step 2:   Introduce the whole induced bias block matrix using the formula

$$
C = BB - nB
$$

$$
= diag\,(A, C4)\, diag\,(A, C4) - diag\,(6, 3)\, diag\,(A, C4):
$$

$$
\begin{array}{ccccccccc}
0 & 3.7619 & 60.0000 & 23.6000 & -8.2667 & -2.1667 & 0 & 0 & 0 \\
4.6500 & 0 & -5.2500 & -7.1500 & 4.6833 & -0.2333 & 0 & 0 & 0 \\
-0.9893 & 1.9952 & 0 & 0.6619 & 0.4841 & 1.4762 & 0 & 0 & 0 \\
-1.8333 & 8.7143 & -7.6667 & 0 & 0.1778 & 6.8333 & 0 & 0 & 0 \\
3.3333 & -14.6190 & 39.0000 & 21.3333 & 0 & -4.5000 & 0 & 0 & 0 \\
4.3611 & 0.5238 & 0.4167 & -7.2167 & 3.8167 & 0 & 0 & 0 & 0 \\
0 & 0 & 0 & 0 & 0 & 0 & 0 & 26.0000 & -5.2000 \\
0 & 0 & 0 & 0 & 0 & 0 & 0.0825 & 0 & 0.5778 \\
0 & 0 & 0 & 0 & 0 & 0 & 0.4127 & -3.7143 & 0
\end{array}
$$

Step 3:   The elements with largest absolute values in the sub-matrices A and C4 are 60 and 26 respectively, which are located at 1st row and 3rd column, 7th row and 8th column, respectively.

Step 4:   The vectors are

$$
r_1 = \begin{pmatrix} 1 & 4 & 3 & 1 & 3 & 4 & 0 & 0 & 0 \end{pmatrix} \quad \text{and}
$$

$$
c_3^T = \begin{pmatrix} 3 & 7 & 1 & 5 & 5 & 6 & 0 & 0 & 0 \end{pmatrix}
$$

$$
r_7 = \begin{pmatrix} 0 & 0 & 0 & 0 & 0 & 0 & 1 & 9 & 7 \end{pmatrix} \quad \text{and}
$$

$$
c_8^T = \begin{pmatrix} 0 & 0 & 0 & 0 & 0 & 0 & 9 & 1 & 5 \end{pmatrix}
$$

Step 5:   The scalar products b are

$$
b_1 = r_1 \cdot c_3^T = \begin{pmatrix} 3 & 28 & 3 & 5 & 15 & 24 & 0 & 0 & 0 \end{pmatrix}
$$

$$
b_2 = r_7 \cdot c_8^T = \begin{pmatrix} 0 & 0 & 0 & 0 & 0 & 0 & 9 & 9 & 35 \end{pmatrix}
$$

Step 6: The bias identifying vectors f are

$$f_1 = r_1 \cdot c_3^T - b_{13} = \left(0\ 25\ 0\ 2\ 12\ 21\ -3\ -3\ -3\right)$$

$$f_2 = r_7 \cdot c_8^T - b_{78} = \left(-9\ -9\ -9\ -9\ -9\ -9\ 0\ 0\ 26\right)$$

Step 7: From the scalar products b_1 and b_2 and the bias identifying vectors f_1 and f_2, we can find that the inconsistent values are $b_{12}b_{23} = 28$ and $b_{79}b_{98} = 35$, which are corresponding the inconsistent elements $A_{12}A_{23} = 28$ and $C3_{13}C3_{32} = 35$. Besides, since there are three elements in f_1 far away from b_{13}, therefore, the corresponding a_{13} might be too small.

Furthermore, $c_{12} = 3.7619 > 0$, $c_{23} = -5.25 < 0$, $c_{79} = -5.2 < 0$, $c_{98} = -3.7143 < 0$ and $c_{13} = 60 > 0$. These inequalities indicate that the value of b_{12} is too small; the value of b_{23} is too large; the values of b_{79} and b_{98} are probably too large, respectively. Besides, the value of $b_{79}b_{98}$ is supposed to be 9 or close to 9 instead of 35. That is, the value of a_{12} is small; the value of a_{23} is too large; the values of $c3_{13}$ and $c3_{32}$ are possible too large and a_{13} is too small. Those elements should be revised. For instance, Let:

$$a_{13} = 9,\ a_{31} = \frac{1}{9},\quad a_{23} = 3,\ a_{32} = \frac{1}{3}$$

$$c3_{13} = 2,\ c3_{31} = \frac{1}{2}\quad c3_{32} = 4,\ c3_{23} = \frac{1}{4}$$

The values of the elements in the sub-matrix A and sub-matrix C3 are replaced with the above corresponding values of elements and calculate their maximum eigenvalues to test the consistency. That is:

The maximum eigenvalues are $\lambda^0{}_{max} = 7.1374$ and $\lambda^4{}_{max} = 3.0246$.

Test the consistencies using the maximum eigenvalue threshold method.

$$\lambda^0{}_{max} = \lambda^0{}_{max} - \lambda^6{}_{lim\,max} = 7.1374 - 6.781 = 0.3564 > 0$$

$$\Delta\lambda^4{}_{max} = \lambda^3{}_{max} - \lambda^3{}_{lim\,max} = 3.0246 - 3.104 = -0.0794 < 0$$

The comparison matrix C4 passed the consistency test, however, the comparison matrix A is still inconsistent. Identify the inconsistent elements in the comparison matrix A using the second largest bias value 39, the third largest bias value 23.6, and the fourth largest bias value 21.3333. These three elements are located at 5th row and 3rd column, 1st row and 4th column, 5th row and 4th column, respectively. Repeat the above steps, the corresponding bias identifying vector f_i $(i = 1, 2, 3)$ becomes:

$$f_1 = r_5 \cdot c_3^T - b_{53} = \begin{pmatrix} -4 & 30 & 0 & 0 & 0 & 13 & -5 & -5 & -5 \end{pmatrix}$$

$$f_2 = r_1 \cdot c_4^T - b_{14} = \begin{pmatrix} 0 & 11 & -0.4 & 0 & 2 & 11 & -1 & -1 & -1 \end{pmatrix}$$

$$f_3 = r_5 \cdot c_4^T - b_{54} = \begin{pmatrix} -0.6667 & 14 & 0 & 0 & 0 & 8 & -1 & -1 & -1 \end{pmatrix}$$

From the above three bias identifying vectors f_1, f_2 and f_3, we can find that the inconsistent values are:

In f_1 : $b_{52}b_{23} = 35$ and $b_{56}b_{63} = 18$ $\Leftrightarrow$ $a_{52}a_{23} = 35$ and $a_{56}a_{63} = 18$ in matrix A

In f_2 : $b_{12}b_{24} = 11$ and $b_{16}b_{64} = 11$ $\Leftrightarrow$ $a_{12}a_{24} = 11$ and $a_{16}a_{64} = 11$ in matrix A

In f_3 : $b_{52}b_{24} = 14$ and $b_{56}b_{64} = 8$ $\Leftrightarrow$ $a_{52}a_{24} = 14$ and $a_{56}a_{64} = 8$ in matrix A

where the symbol ' $\Leftrightarrow$ ' denotes "corresponding to".
The following inequalities show the inconsistent elements:

$$c_{52} = -14.619 < 0 \Rightarrow a_{52} \text{ is too large}$$

$$c_{23} = -5.25 < 0 \quad \Rightarrow a_{23} \text{ is too large}$$

$$c_{56} = -4.5 < 0 \quad \Rightarrow a_{56} \text{ is too large}$$

$$c_{63} = 0.41675 > 0 \Rightarrow a_{63} \text{ is slightly small}$$

$$c_{12} = 3.7619 > 0 \quad \Rightarrow a_{12} \text{ is too small}$$

$$c_{24} = -7.15 < 0 \quad \Rightarrow a_{24} \text{ is too large}$$

$$c_{16} = -2.1667 < 0 \Rightarrow a_{16} \text{ is too large}$$

$$c_{64} = -7.2167 < 0 \Rightarrow a_{64} \text{ is too large}$$

For instance, decrease the values of the three elements with largest absolute value a_{52}, a_{24} and a_{64}. Let

$$a_{52} = 1, \ a_{25} = 1; \quad a_{24} = 1/2, \ a_{42} = 2; \quad a_{64} = 1/2, \ a_{64} = 2$$

Replace all the corresponding values in the original comparison matrix A with the above values and calculate the maximum value of matrix A, we can get $\lambda_{max}^0 = 6.6156 < \lambda_{max\,thrd}^6 = 6.781$. The comparison matrix passes the consistency test. If the inconsistent elements identified in the first time, a_{13} and a_{23}, are replace with $a_{13} = 9$, $a_{31} = \frac{1}{9}$, $a_{23} = 3$, $a_{32} = \frac{1}{3}$, and continue to calculate the maximum eigenvalue of comparison matrix A, then $\lambda_{max}^0 = 6.3174 < \lambda_{max\,thrd}^6 = 6.781$. The comparison matrix A passes the consistency test with smaller maximum eigenvalue, which is corresponding to the small CR.

References

Aguilar-Lasserre AA, Bautista Bautista MA, Ponsich A, Gonzalez Huerta MA (2009) An AHP-based decision-making tool for the solution of multiproduct batch plant design problem under imprecise demand. Comput Oper Res 36(3):711–736

Bonano EJ, Apostolakis GE, Salter PF, Ghassemi A, Jennings S (2000) Application of risk assessment and decision analysis to the evaluation, ranking and selection of environmental remediation alternatives. J Hazard Mat 71(1–3):35–37

Buyya R, Chee SY, Venugopal S, Roberg J, Brandic I (2009) Cloud computing and emerging IT platforms: vision, hype, and reality for delivering computing as the 5th utility. Fut Gener Comput Syst 25(6):599–616

Ergu D, Kou G, Peng Y, Shi Y (2011a) A new consistency index for comparison matrices in the ANP, New State of MCDM in the 21st Century. Lecture notes in economics and mathematical systems, vol 648, part 1, pp 47–56

Ergu D, Kou G, Peng Y, Shi Y (2011b) A simple method to improve the consistency ratio of the pair-wise comparison matrix in ANP. Eur J Oper Res 213(1):246–259. doi:10.1016/j.ejor.2011.03.014

Ergu D, Kou G, Peng Y, Shi Y, Shi Yu (2011d) The analytic hierarchy process: task scheduling and resource allocation in cloud computing environment. J Supercomput. doi:10.1007/s11227-011-0625-1

Ergu D, Kou G, Shi Y, Shi Yu (2011e) Analytic network process in risk assessment and decision analysis. Comput Oper Res. doi:10.1016/j.cor.2011.03.005

Fang YQ, Wang F, Ge JW (2010) Task scheduling algorithm based on load balancing in cloud computing. In: Web information systems and mining lecture notes in computer science, 2010, vol 6318/2010, pp 271–277, doi: 10.1007/978-3-642-16515-3_34

Fujiwara I, Aida K, Ono I (2009) Market-based resource allocation for distributed computing. IPSJ SIG technical report, vol 2009-HPC-121, no. 34,http://www.alab.ip.titech.ac.jp/papers/swopp2009-fujiwara.pdf

Hämäläinen RP, Lindstedt MRK, Sinkko K (2000) Multiattribute risk analysis in nuclear emergency management. Risk Anal 20:455–468. doi:10.1111/0272-4332.204044

Hayes B (2008) Cloud computing. Commun ACM 51(7):9–11

Hu G, Rao K, Sun Z (2007) Identification of a detailed function list for public health emergency management using three qualitative methods. Chin Med J 120(21):1908–1913

Huang YF, Chao BW (2001) A priority-based resource allocation strategy in distributed computing networks. J Syst Software 58(3):221–233

Ismail L, Mills B, Hennebelle A (2008) A formal model of dynamic resource allocation in grid computing environment.http://www.irml.uaeu.ac.ae/hpgcl/images/Publications/snpd2008.pdf.

Khadam IM, Kaluarachchi JJ (2003) Multi-criteria decision analysis with probabilistic risk assessment for the management of contaminated ground water. Environ Impact Assess Rev 23(6):683–721

Koole G, Righter R (2007) Resource allocation in grid computing. J Schedul. doi:10.1007/s10951-007-0018-8

Krewski D, Andersen ME, Mantus E, Zeise L (2009) Reply to invited commentaries on toxicity testing in the 21st century: implications for human health risk assessment. Risk Anal 29:492–497. doi:10.1111/j.1539-6924.2009.01218.x

Linkov I, Satterstrom FK, Kiker G, Batchelor C, Bridges T, Ferguson E (2006) From comparative risk assessment to multi-criteria decision analysis and adaptive management: recent developments and applications. Environ Int 32(8):1072–1093

Moschakis I, Karatza H (2010) Evaluation of gang scheduling performance and cost in a cloud computing system. J Supercomput 59(2):975–992. doi:10.1007/s11227-010-0481-4

Peng Y, Kou G, Shi Y, Chen Z (2008) A descriptive framework for the field of data mining and knowledge discovery. Int J Inf Technol Decis Mak 7(4):639–682

Peng Y, Kou G, Wang G, Wu W, Shi Y (2011a) Ensemble of software defect predictors: an AHP-based evaluation method. Int J Inf Technol Decis Mak 10(1):187–206

Peng Y, Wang G, Kou G, Shi Y (2011b) An empirical performance metric for classification algorithm selection in financial risk management. Appl Soft Comput 11(2):2906–2915

Peng Y, Kou G, Wang G, Shi Y (2011c) FAMCDM: a fusion approach of MCDM methods to rank multiclass classification algorithms. Omega. doi:10.1016/j.omega.2011.01.009

Reckhow KH (1994) Water quality simulation modeling and uncertainty analysis for risk assessment and decision making. Ecol Model 72(1–2):1–20

Saaty TL (1990) How to make a decision: the analytic hierarchy process. Eur J Oper Res 48(1):9–26

Saaty TL (1993) The analytic hierarchy process: a 1993 overview. In: The international workshop on multicriteria decision making. Methods, Algorithms, Applications, Celákovice

Saaty TL (2008) The analytic network process. Iran J Oper Res 1(1):1–27

Saaty TL, Zoffer HJ (2011) Negotiating the Israeli-Palestinian controversy from a new perspective. Int J Inf Technol Decis Mak 10(1):5–64

Triantaphyllou E, Mann SH (1995) Using the analytic hierarchy process for decision making in engineering applications: Some challenges. Int J Ind Eng Appl Pract 2(1):35–44

Wagner MR, Bhadury J, Peng S (2009) Risk management in uncapacitated facility location models with random demands. Comput Oper Res 36(4):1002–1011

Wei G, Vasilakos AV, Zheng Y, Xiong N (2009) A game-theoretic method of fair resource allocation for cloud computing services. J Supercomput 54(2):252–269. doi:10.1007/s11227-009-0318-1

Wijnmalen DJD (2007) Analysis of benefits, opportunities, costs, and risks (BOCR) with the AHP-ANP: a critical validation. Math Comput Model 46(7–8):892–905

Yazır YO, Matthews C, Farahbod R, Neville S, Guitouni A, Ganti S, Coady Y (2010) Dynamic resource allocation in computing clouds through distributed multiple criteria decision analysis. In: IEEE 3rd international conference on Cloud Computing, 5–10 July, pp 91–98

Chapter 8
Induced Arithmetic Average Bias Matrix Model (IAABMM)

In previous Chapters, IBMM and its related extensions and applications are presented. In Ergu and Kou (2012), another form of induced bias matrix model, induced arithmetic average bias matrix model (IAABMM), is proposed and proved mathematically, which is easier to be understood than the previous model. In addition, two simpler inconsistency identification processes are also analyzed and proposed. An estimating formula of inconsistency adjustment for IAABMM is derived for the first time and illustrated by two numerical examples. In this Chapter, the details of IAABMM will be described.

8.1   The Theorem of IAABMM

To effectively identify the inconsistent elements while preserving most of the original information in a PCM, the arithmetic average bias is induced in this paper. The proposed theorem is described below.

Theorem 8.1. *If the PCM A is perfectly (or approximately) consistent, then the induced arithmetic average bias matrix C should be (or close) zeroes. That is, the following induced bias matrix holds:*

$$C = \frac{1}{n}AA - A = (c_{ij}) \begin{cases} = 0 & if\ a_{ik}a_{kj} = a_{ij} \\ \approx 0 & if\ a_{ik}a_{kj} \approx a_{ij} \end{cases} \tag{8.1}$$

where A is the original PCM, n is the order of A, while $c_{ij} = \frac{1}{n}\sum_{k=1}^{n} a_{ik}a_{kj} - a_{ij}$ is the induced arithmetic average bias.

Proofs. If the PCM $A = (a_{ij})_{n \times n}$ is perfectly consistent, that is, $a_{ik}a_{kj} = a_{ij}$ for all $i, j\ and\ k$. Then,

$$c_{ij} = \frac{1}{n}\sum_{k=1}^{n} a_{ik}a_{kj} - a_{ij} = \frac{1}{n}\sum_{k=1}^{n} a_{ij} - a_{ij} = \frac{1}{n}na_{ij} - a_{ij} = 0$$

Therefore, the induced arithmetic average bias matrix C is a zero matrix if matrix A is perfectly consistent. The equality symbol "=" is replaced by the approximated symbol "$\approx$", then the approximately consistent case can easily be proved.

Corollary 8.1. *If matrix A is inconsistent, then the induced arithmetic average bias matrix C cannot be zeros. More precisely, there is at least one entry in i^{th} row or column of matrix C greater than 0.*

Proofs. If matrix A is inconsistent, $a_{ij} \neq a_{ik}a_{kj}$ holds at least for one of the i, j, k ($i, j, k = 1, 2, \cdots, n$). Specifically, for any i, there exist j and k such that $a_{ij} \neq a_{ik}a_{kj}$. Saaty (1980) also proved that for the maximal eigenvalue λ_{max} of A, $\lambda_{max} \geq n$, and matrix A is consistent if and only if $\lambda_{max} = n$. Namely, $\lambda_{max} > n$ if matrix A is inconsistent. In addition, the corresponding unique eigenvector ω_{max} is a positive vector.

Applying the following equation to matrix C

$$A\omega_{max} = \lambda_{max}\omega_{max} \tag{8.2}$$

We get

$$C\omega_{max} = \left(\frac{1}{n}AA - A\right)\omega_{max} = \frac{1}{n}AA\omega_{max} - A\omega_{max}$$

$$= \frac{1}{n}A\lambda_{max}\omega_{max} - \lambda_{max}\omega_{max} = \frac{1}{n}\lambda_{max}^2\omega_{max} - \lambda_{max}\omega_{max}$$

$$= \frac{1}{n}\lambda_{max}(\lambda_{max} - n)\omega_{max} \tag{8.3}$$

Since $\lambda_{max} > n$, $C\omega_{max}$ is a positive vector. Consequently, C cannot have any row containing only zeros. More precisely, any row of C must contain at least one positive element.

8.2   The Inconsistency Identification Processes of IAABMM

Based on the *Corollary 8.1*, the inconsistent element can be identified by observing and analyzing the absolute largest value in matrix C. The processes of inconsistency identification proposed in Ergu et al. (2011b) can be used to identify the inconsistent element in this model. A new way of inconsistency identification is proposed in the following.

The Principle of Inconsistency Identification

In the proposed model $C = AA/n - A$, if the inconsistent element is identified firstly through analyzing the absolute largest value denoted as $c_{ij}^{\max}$ in the matrix C, then we get

$$c_{ij}^{\max} = \frac{1}{n} \sum_{k=1}^{n} a_{ik}a_{kj} - a_{ij} \tag{8.4}$$

If the $c_{ij}^{\max}$ is positive, the first term of Eq. (8.4) is greater than a_{ij}, usually indicating the arithmetic average of $a_{ik}a_{kj}(k = 1, 2, \cdots, n)$ is greater than a_{ij}, which can be caused by any of a_{ik} or a_{kj}. Sometimes it is caused by a_{ij} because it is too small. So we need to create the ith row or j^{th} column to further identify the inconsistent element using the vector dot product method, which could be complicated. Details are referred to Ergu et al. (2011b). However, if a_{ij} is the inconsistent element, here assume it is larger than $\frac{1}{n} \sum_{k=1}^{n} a_{ik}a_{kj}$ (if it is too small, then we can find another inconsistent element a_{ji} that would be too large since they are reciprocal), then $c_{ij} = \frac{1}{n} \sum_{k=1}^{n} a_{ik}a_{kj} - a_{ij}$ must be the negative largest value, denoted as $c_{ij}^{-\max}$. Conversely, $c_{ji} = \frac{1}{n} \sum_{k=1}^{n} a_{jk}a_{ki} - a_{ji}$ must be far away from zero and be positive. Therefore, the principle of inconsistency identification is to observe firstly the negative largest value in matrix C, denoted as $c_{ij}^{-\max}$, then the corresponding element in matrix A, a_{ij}, probably is the inconsistent elements.

The specific principles of inconsistency identification include: (1) if the $c_{ij}^{-\max}$ is far greater than the other negative bias elements, and its corresponding bias element c_{ji} is positive and larger than zero, then a_{ij} can be identified as the inconsistent element; (2) If there are some negative bias elements c_{kl}, c_{mn}, c_{pq} in matrix C that are close to the $c_{ij}^{-\max}$, then create bias pairs using their reciprocal values, and analyze their absolute bias values and distributions. The elements with largest absolute bias as well as relatively symmetric distribution with respect to the reference point zero are regarded as the inconsistent elements.

For instance, assume the closest negative largest bias elements aforementioned and their reciprocals are,

(a) $\left(c_{ij}^{-\max}, c_{ji}\right) = (-4.3, \ 1.3)$;   (b) $(c_{kl}, c_{lk}) = (-3.6, \ 1.8)$

(c) $(c_{mn}, c_{nm}) = (-3.4, \ 0.13)$;   (d) $\left(c_{pq}, c_{qp}\right) = (-3.1, \ 1.1)$

Their absolute bias values are.

(a)' $\Delta c_{ij} = \left|c_{ij}^{-\max} - c_{ji}\right| = 5.6$;   (b)' $\Delta c_{kl} = |c_{kl} - c_{lk}| = 5.4$

(c)' $\Delta c_{mn} = |c_{mn} - c_{nm}| = 3.53$;   (d)' $\Delta c_{pq} = \left|c_{pq} - c_{qp}\right| = 4.2$

Although $\Delta c_{ij} = 5.6$ is larger than $\Delta c_{kl} = 5.4$, the distribution of Δc_{kl} is relatively more symmetric than that of Δc_{ij} with respect to the reference point zero, indicating that the corresponding element a_{ij} is too large, but its reciprocal a_{ij} is not too mall. However, the corresponding element c_{lk} is large, and its reciprocal element c_{kl} is too small. Therefore, the element c_{kl} can be identified as the most inconsistent element.

The Processes of Inconsistency Identification and Adjustment

The specific steps of inconsistency identification and adjustment include:

Step I: Inconsistency identification

Step 1: Construct the induced bias matrix C using $C = \frac{1}{n}AA - A$
Step 2: Observe the negative largest bias values in matrix C
Step 3: Identify the inconsistent elements using the identification method afore-mentioned.

Step II: Inconsistency adjustment

Step 1: Calculate the inconsistent element using the estimating formula (8.5) (see Sect. 8.3)
Step 2: Test the consistency of the revised matrix A by replacing the inconsistent elements with the estimated values.

8.3   The Estimating Formula of Inconsistency Adjustment

When the inconsistent elements are identified, the decision makers are asked to revise their judgments to improve the consistency ratio. However, it is sometimes time-consuming and consumed high cost as well as delaying the decision making. Therefore, it is necessary to derive a formula to estimate the possible value for the identified inconsistent elements. Assume the identified inconsistent element in matrix A is a_{ij}, then the value of a_{ij} can be estimated by analyzing the formula of c_{ij} in the induced bias matrix C. Since a_{ij} is inconsistent, $a_{ij} \neq a_{ik}a_{kj}$. Suppose $a_{ik}a_{kj} = a'_{ij} \ (k \neq i, j)$, then

$$c_{ij} = \frac{1}{n}\sum_{k=1}^{n} a_{ik}a_{kj} - a_{ij} = \frac{1}{n}[2a_{ij}+(n-2)a'_{ij}] - a_{ij} \tag{8.5}$$

From Eq. (8.5), the value of a'_{ij} can be derived,

$$a'_{ij} = \frac{nc_{ij} + (n-2)a_{ij}}{n-2} = \frac{n}{n-2}c_{ij} + a_{ij} \tag{8.6}$$

Therefore, the value of inconsistent element a_{ij} can be estimated by the value of a'_{ij}, as shown in (8.6). The effectiveness of the proposed method and the estimating formula of inconsistent element are illustrated by two numerical examples in the following section.

Likewise, the estimating formula of inconsistent element in the model $C = AA - nA$ can also be derived. Details are shown below.

$$c_{ij} = \sum_{k=1}^{n} a_{ik}a_{kj} - na_{ij} = 2a_{ij} + \sum_{\substack{k=1 \\ \neq i,j}}^{n} a_{ik}a_{kj} - na_{ij} = [2a_{ij}+(n-2)a'_{ij}] - na_{ij}$$

$$(8.7)$$

$$a'_{ij} = \frac{c_{ij} + (n-2)a_{ij}}{n-2} = \frac{1}{n-2}c_{ij} + a_{ij} \qquad (8.8)$$

Formula (8.8) can be used to estimate the identified inconsistent elements when IBMM is used.

8.4   Illustrative Examples

To illustrate the proposed model and demonstrate the processes of inconsistency identification and adjustment proposed in Sects. 8.2 and 8.3, the *Examples 1 and 2* introduced in Ergu et al. (2011b) is used as *Examples 8.2 and 8.1* in this paper.

Example 8.1. The 8×8 pair-wise comparison matrix A first used in Ergu et al. (2011b) as *Example 2* is slightly inconsistent with $CR = 0.1055 > 0.1$ or $\lambda_{\max} = 9.0339 > \lambda_{thrd}^{8} = 8.89\,(\Delta\lambda_{\max} = 0.1439 > 0)$.

$$A = \begin{bmatrix} 1 & 2 & 1/2 & 2 & 1/2 & 2 & 1/2 & 2 \\ 1/2 & 1 & 4 & 1 & 1/4 & 1 & 1/4 & 1 \\ 2 & 1/4 & 1 & 4 & 1 & 4 & 1 & 4 \\ 1/2 & 1 & 1/4 & 1 & 1/4 & 1 & 1/4 & 1 \\ 2 & 4 & 1 & 4 & 1 & 4 & 1 & 4 \\ 1/2 & 1 & 1/4 & 1 & 1/4 & 1 & 1/4 & 1 \\ 2 & 4 & 1 & 4 & 1 & 4 & 1 & 4 \\ 1/2 & 1 & 1/4 & 1 & 1/4 & 1 & 1/4 & 1 \end{bmatrix}$$

Apply the proposed model to this matrix, details are as follows.

Step I: Inconsistency identification

Step 1: Construct the induced bias matrix C using $C = \frac{1}{n}AA - A$

$$
C = \begin{pmatrix}
0 & -0.2344 & 0.9375 & 0 & 0 & 0 & 0 & 0 \\
0.9375 & 0 & -2.8125 & 1.8750 & 0.4688 & 1.8750 & 0.4688 & 1.8750 \\
-0.2344 & 2.8125 & 0 & -0.4688 & -0.1172 & -0.4688 & -0.1172 & -0.4688 \\
0 & -0.1172 & 0.4688 & 0 & 0 & 0 & 0 & 0 \\
0 & -0.4688 & 1.8750 & 0 & 0 & 0 & 0 & 0 \\
0 & -0.1172 & 0.4688 & 0 & 0 & 0 & 0 & 0 \\
0 & -0.4688 & 1.8750 & 0 & 0 & 0 & 0 & 0 \\
0 & -0.1172 & 0.4688 & 0 & 0 & 0 & 0 & 0
\end{pmatrix}
$$

Step 2: Observe the negative largest bias values $c_{ij}^{-\max}$ in matrix C. Here, there is only one element with largest bias value, $c_{23}^{-\max} = -2.8125$.

Step 3: Identify the inconsistent elements using the identification method. Since there is only one element with negative largest bias value, $c_{23}^{-\max} = -2.8125$, and its reciprocal is $c_{23} = 2.8125$, therefore, the corresponding element a_{23} is identified as the inconsistent elements.

Step II: Inconsistency adjustment

Step 1: Calculate the inconsistent element a_{23} using the estimating formula (8.8) (see Sect. 8.3)

$$
a'_{23} = \frac{n}{n-2} c_{23} + a_{23} = \frac{8}{6}(-2.8125) + 4 = \frac{1}{4}
$$

Step 2: Test the consistency of the revised matrix A by replacing the a_{23} and a_{32} with 1/4 and 4. We can get that $\lambda_{\max} = 8$, and CR $= 0$.

Example 8.2. To illustrate such case that there are several negative large bias elements in matrix C, the *Example 8.1* used in Ergu et al. (2011b) is again introduced in this paper. The 4×4 pair-wise comparison matrix A is inconsistent with CR $= 0.173 > 0.1$ or $\lambda_{\max} = 4.4644 > \lambda_{thrd}^{4} = 4.267$ ($\Delta\lambda_{\max} = 0.1974 > 0$).

$$
A = \begin{pmatrix}
1 & 1/9 & 3 & 1/5 \\
9 & 1 & 5 & 2 \\
1/3 & 1/5 & 1 & 1/2 \\
5 & 1/2 & 2 & 1
\end{pmatrix}
$$

Apply the proposed model to this matrix, we have:

Step I: Inconsistency identification

Step 1: Construct the induced bias matrix C using $C = \frac{1}{n}AA - A$

$$
C = \begin{pmatrix}
0 & 0.1194 & -1.2611 & 0.3306 \\
-1.5833 & 0 & 5.2500 & 0.0750 \\
0.9083 & -0.0282 & 0 & -0.1333 \\
-1.2083 & -0.0111 & 3.3750 & 0
\end{pmatrix}
$$

Step 2: The negative largest bias values $c_{ij}^{-\max}$ in matrix C are $c_{21}^{-\max} = -1.5833$, $c_{13} = -1.2611$ and $c_{41} = -1.2083$.

Step 3: Identify the inconsistent elements using the absolute bias value and their distribution method. We have

(1) $\left(c_{21}^{-\max}, c_{12}\right) = (-1.5833, 0.1194)$; (2) $(c_{13}, c_{31}) = (-1.2611, 0.9083)$,

(3) $(c_{41}, c_{14}) = (-1.2083, 0.3306)$;

Their absolute bias values are.

(1)'. $\Delta c_{21} = |c_{21}^{-\max} - c_{12}| = 1.7027$; (2)'. $\Delta c_{13} = |c_{13} - c_{31}| = 2.1694$,

(3)'. $\Delta c_{41} = |c_{41} - c_{14}| = 1.5389$;

Although c_{21} has the negative largest bias value, its reciprocal c_{12}, 0.1194, is too small, which is close to zero. It is shown that the corresponding element a_{21} is not the inconsistent element. However, Δc_{13} is largest absolute bias value, and the distribution of $(c_{13}, c_{31}) = (-1.2611, 0.9083)$ is relative symmetric with respect to the reference point zero. Therefore, the corresponding element a_{13} is identified as the inconsistent elements.

Step II: Inconsistency adjustment

Step 1: Calculate the inconsistent element a_{13} using the estimating formula (8.8) (see Sect. 8.3)

$$a'_{13} = \frac{n}{n-2}c_{13} + a_{13} = \frac{4}{2}(-1.2611) + 3 = 0.4778 \approx \frac{1}{2}$$

Step 2: Test the consistency of the revised matrix A by replacing the a_{13} and a_{31} with 1/2 and 2. We can get that $\lambda_{\max} = 4.0076$, and $C.R. = 0.0028 < 0.1$. Therefore, the revised matrix passed the consistency test.

In the above two examples, the identified inconsistent elements and their estimated value are the same ones calculated by the model $C = AA - nA$ in Ergu et al. (2011b) but the processes of inconsistency identification and adjustment are simpler and easier.

References

Ergu D, Kou G (2012) IAABM for consistency test in pairwise comparison matrix. Information

Ergu D, Kou G, Peng Y, Shi Y (2011b) A simple method to improve the consistency ratio of the pair-wise comparison matrix in ANP. Eur J Oper Res 213(1):246–259. doi:10.1016/j.ejor.2011.03.014

Saaty TL (1980) The analytical hierarchy process. McGraw-Hill, New York

G. Kou et al., *Data Processing for the AHP/ANP*, Quantitative Management 1,
DOI 10.1007/978-3-642-29213-2, © Springer-Verlag Berlin Heidelberg 2013

Index